NEW WORLD

CIRCUMSTANTIAL VICTIM
INSTIGATOR
LADYBIRD

Three Plays

by
ARTHUR EGBUNIWE

TRAFFORD

National Library of Canada Cataloguing in Publication

Egbuniwe, Arthur
New world / Arthur Egbuniwe.

Plays.
ISBN 1-55395-200-6

I. Title.
PR9095.9.E42N48 2002 822'.92 C2002-904885-0

TRAFFORD

This book was published *on-demand* in cooperation with Trafford Publishing.

On-demand publishing is a unique process and service of making a book available for retail sale to the public taking advantage of on-demand manufacturing and Internet marketing. **On-demand publishing** includes promotions, retail sales, manufacturing, order fulfilment, accounting and collecting royalties on behalf of the author.

Suite 6E, 2333 Government St., Victoria, B.C. V8T 4P4, CANADA
Phone 250-383-6864 Toll-free 1-888-232-4444 Can/US
Fax 250-383-6804 E-mail sales@trafford.com
Website www.trafford.com

TRAFFORD PUBLISHING IS A DIVISION OF TRAFFORD HOLDINGS LTD.

Trafford Catalogue #02-0914 www.trafford.com/robots/02-0914.html

10 9 8 7 6 5 4 3 2

I dedicate this book to God Almighty for all the good things that he has done for me. His grace and goodness are what keeps me going. Also to my wife Monika Hirzabauer, my son Noel, my daughter Afoma, and my whole family. And to my friend Christoph Weritsch, who is always there for me, Mrs. Veada Stoff, Mike & Natascha and others too numerous to mention here. I appreciate all the encouragement I received from all of you.

PROLOGUE

This book is not a direct reflection of any particular person or place, but rather it relates to our everyday lives. It's just an imaginary reflection of what is or might be taking place around us. As we move forward in life, we should try to treat everybody we meet with an open mind because you never know who can be your guardian angel. We should never write people off because of their looks or where they come from, and we should never let race be a judgmental factor in our assessment of people. May God bless you all.

NEW WORLD

CONTENTS

Three Plays

CIRCUMSTANTIAL VICTIM

A Play

CHAPTER ONE

The boys of house number seven finish their morning routine and all go to work in various directions, but usually they all gather again at the rolling park after the day's work to relax, talk about their various problems back home, and later they end up playing football.

It's four o'clock on a nice Saturday afternoon. Jones and Santos have both finished their work for the day, and they are at the park discussing things with a few other boys. Jones and Santos decide to take a walk around the park.

SANTOS: Jones, why don't we take a walk while we wait for Oliveria to show up.

JONES: Boy, you always look like you feel very happy after doing that job. I wonder what it's like way back in your country, what makes you so happy to do this menial work. Look, don't you feel that job is meant for a robot, that you are like a slave to your employer?

SANTOS: Why talk this way as if there is a better job for us to do and we can choose to do this one or not do this one? Look, the fact is we must do this as a means of supplementing the little support we get from the state. Do you know of any other way to get financial help to support yourself, other than something against the law, of course, because crime don't pay.

JONES: Look Santos, why all this shit about crime?

Have I ever told you I am going into a life of crime, and even if I do it's my business so don't preach this anti-crime stuff to me. Mr. Good Attitude, always wanting to be the good guy.

SANTOS: Look, why get so upset over this. I don't mean to call you a criminal, if it upset you. I'm sorry. But you should think how life is way back in your country, how it was before the political turmoil at least. Now you are doing far better, and you are safe from political crisis so why not thank God for that and feel happy? Why be thinking about how to get rich? Quick money is not everything that matters in this life. After all you don't have it back home in your country. So stop all the fuss about a better paying job or thinking of other means of getting money.

JONES: Hey, don't give me that shit about my country and my condition in my country, okay! I must find something else to do.

SANTOS: Please don't do anything against the law, okay? That's all I'm asking.

JONES: I told you, don't preach this anti-crime line to me, okay Mr. Good Guy?

SANTOS: Sorry, it's okay. Look, that's Fidelis Oliveria coming.

[*And from the distance, Oliveria shouts:*]

OLIVERIA: Hi guys! Why don't we play some football?

JONES: Aren't you tired after doing that paper job? I wonder what it's like way back in your country.

SANTOS: Hey, mind your language! My country is blessed with hard-working, God-fearing people who are content with what they get.

JONES: Okay Mr. Good Country guys, let's play ball.

OLIVERIA: Tomorrow is Sunday. I hope we will all be going to church.

SANTOS: Sure.

JONES: Boy, I don't like the religious doctrine here,

and besides it's always better to sit at home and pray to God if he wants.

SANTOS: You choose to be totally the opposite of everyone else in everything, even in religious matters.

OLIVERIA: Santos, look, everybody has their own views on life, and you two guys have been arguing about everything of late.

SANTOS: Oliveria, I think Jones has been drinking and smoking so he can say all things are the opposite of what they should be.

JONES: Sorry Mr., but I do drink and I do smoke, but do you think that not doing these things will give you a passport to heaven?

OLIVERIA: Hey guys, stop this argument! Let's just join the others on the field of play.

[*They played with the rest for one hour and everybody was tired and ready to go home.*

Oliveria looks at his watch and says to the rest of guys of "House 7":]

JONES: Guys of the "house," look it's late. We all better rush so that the Mr. Dandy the chef won't punish us for arriving late.

JONES: Look boy, don't hurry us! If Mr. Dandy doesn't like us to be late, he should kick us out if we are late. Who cares for a drink? Let's go have a drink and a smoke. What kind of a house is it where there is no drinking and no smoking.

SANTOS: Oliveria, I'm off to the house. Who cares to come along?

JONES: Bye! See you later, Mr. Good Guys.

[*Back in the house the boys have finished their evening food and are cooling off in the dining room, watching television and playing cards. Mr. Dandy is in his office, checking the list in the computer he finds out that Jones and two other boys have yet to come back. He checks his watch and it's 9.45. Suddenly there is a knock on the door.*]

Dandy: Yes! Who is it?

Jones: It's us, Mr. Dandy.

Dandy: "Us" is not a name.

Jones: It's Mr. Jones and Mr. Oliveria.

Dandy [*opens the door and asks them into his office*]: What kept you so late? You were to be in some time ago.

Jones: We took a walk with a nice girl from down the road. We are sorry we came late.

Dandy: I know you will have a ready-made answer to any question at any time. I guess the girls took you home and gave you some drinks as well.

Jones: They ask us to come in for coffee and we ended up drinking.

Dandy: Just make sure you are not late next time. Go on into the dining room and find yourself something to eat.

[*Back in the dining Jones say hi to the guys.*]

Jones: Santos, you won't believe it. We met some nice looking girls and they took us home to drink.

Santos: Just go get something to eat and then get some sleep. That excuse is meant for Mr. Dandy, not for me and the others because I know your usual joint.

Jones: Believe it or not, my words are the truth. What a nice evening! What's going on tomorrow?

Santos: We will be going to church. It's Sunday. You better hurry up to bed so that you will be up early.

Jones: Thank you, papa. I better go to sleep. I must go to sleep, just as my father, Mr. Santos, has just said. Cayston Island is full of character, enough to go around.

Santos: Look, he is dead drunk and he is questioning others' perception of *his* character. I am going to sleep. See you guys in the morning.

[*An hour later, everyone is asleep and Mr. Dandy goes around the house turning out the lights. Early in the morning, Santos and Oliveria are in the shower.*]

SANTOS: Oliveria, did you meet any girls yesterday?

OLIVERIA: Yes, at the joint, but we didn't go to their place. We only made an appointment to meet them there the same time today, but I don't think I'll be going with Jones. Tomorrow is working day. I better go and up Jones. I know he will be sleeping if left alone. [*He goes to Jones' bed and taps his legs.*] Up boy, it's past eight in the morning and we will be going to church this morning.

JONES: Oh this poverty-stricken life that one must wake at a time others declare.

OLIVERIA: Up boy, shower and let's go to church.

JONES: Okay boy. I know if it were Santos waking me, he would want to start of an argument this morning as soon as I open my mouth.

OLIVERIA: Go on into the shower. The water is warm now.

[*They all finish showering and eat their breakfast of tea and bread by 9:45, then they go to church. After the service, they gather outside the church as usual to see if any member will call them for a black job during the week.*]

JONES: Why hangout here waiting for these people who have just preached equality, both in colour and wealth, to look at us as peasants, as beggars looking for help. I used to think the church is a place where brothers give to one another without waiting to be asked.

SANTOS: Why are you talking this way on the church premises? Just think of what God must think of you.

OLIVERIA: You both have a point, but let's end this argument and go home.

JONES: Oliveria, how old do you say you are to talk and behave so maturely? Did you grow up living with your grandparents, taking on their ways from birth?

SANTOS: Jones, did you grow up living with your bachelor uncle all your time back home, learning how to talk and live like you do?

JONES: I won't argue with you. I've got better things to do, like enjoy my Sunday. Let us all go to the park.

[*They all went to the park from there. Jones and a group of other boys left to visit some friends while Santos and Oliveria went back to the house to have a nice Sunday conversation. Jones came back a bit late again in the night looking drunk and went straight to bed.*]

CHAPTER TWO

[*It's seven o'clock in the morning and as usual the chef Mr. Dandy comes to wake everybody up for the day by turning on the light and calling their names. When he gets to the room where Jones sleeps, he turns on the light and calls the names. All get up except Jones.*]

MR. DANDY: Jones, get up. I know you always want to sleep, always wanting the easy way of life. Let me look at your eyes. What have you taken?

JONES: Nothing.

DANDY: I hope that is true.

[*All go to wash and to prepare for breakfast of tea and bread. Oliveria, Santos, and others are already in the dining room waiting. Jones finishes and comes in to join them.*]

JONES: Hey guys, you waiting for Mr. President to eat and get out to work. The only reward from a job is work, hard work. Look, I don't like Mr. Dandy. He's always complaining about my eyes. I don't know what anything I do has got to do with him. Santos, I met some of my countrymen yesterday. Boy, come with me today. I am going to see them. They've invited me for lunch.

SANTOS: Okay, but I hope they are not exactly like you, very contrary and difficult to understand.

JONES: Why talk of guys you've not even seen like this? It is not a fair way to assess them.

SANTOS: I am sorry. It's just a joke.

[*Usually on Monday there is no paper work, so Jones and Santos decide to take a walk along the slope down into the park.*]

JONES: Boy Santos, if you see the kind of cloth and shoes those my town boys are putting on you'll be amazed, not to talk of the way they spend money. Not like your soiled jeans and shirt and off-colour shoes.

SANTOS: Do you know how they got their money? what are they doing? Do they work? And look, try to be contented with what is yours, and mind you, all fingers are not equal.

JONES: I thought your father was a politician, but you talk like the son of a religious teacher. And look, don't preach to me. Our tastes in life are completely different.

SANTOS: Jones, tomorrow there is a meeting in the church. Will you come?

JONES: You suddenly changed our discussion, clever master. Maybe, I will come anyway, just for something to do. Hey, it's two o'clock. Let's go and see my countrymen. They asked me to meet them at McDonalds.

SANTOS: McDonalds? Look, that place is meant for executives, not for people like you and me.

JONES: Look, just behave big when you get there and don't talk because I know you'll mess things up if you do. I want to get to know them, to find out how they got so rich.

SANTOS: I won't talk. It's your people and your business, so it's not my business to intervene. But I tell you, don't think of doing what they do to get their living.

JONES: Let's stop a taxi.

SANTOS: Taxis are expensive.

JONES: I'm paying. I want my countrymen to respect me at least a little. If you present yourself like this, coming on like a tramp and walking down to the place, they will look at you as an ordinary beggar. Look, there is a taxi! Driver, McDonalds.

[*They get in and upon arriving at McDonalds Jones pays the driver 200 straf.*]

SANTOS: That is a very wrong way of life, making people think you are in a class to which you know you don't belong.

JONES: Why all this talk again? Please let's don't argue today.

SANTOS: Boy, that money could have taken us for a bus ride up to one week, and you just spent it in a single taxi ride.

JONES: Feel big! If they ask if you care for cigarette, don't say you don't smoke. Say you're having a terrible cough, so the doctor asked you to stop.

SANTOS: Look, I don't pretend. I like to be myself.

JONES: Okay, there they are on the inner corner.

[*On getting to the table Jones says, "Hi guys." They stand and embrace one another in the brotherly African way. There are four men and two Cayman Island girls around the table.*]

JONES: Meet my friend Santos. He is a cool guy by any standard. Santos, meet Teddy, Tom, Mac and Willy, and the two girls.

TEDDY [*cuts in*]: My girlfriend Branda and Mac's girl Jackly. Why not place your order and also your friend Santos' order. He is so quiet.

JONES: He's sick of late.

Teddy: Sorry, I think it's a change of weather. Africa and inland have different climates. Oh, here is the waitress.

JONES: Frankfurt burger-hot dog and lime whisky.

SANTOS: Hot dog and orange soft drink.

JONES: Hey Santos, why not take a bit of alcohol. I think it will wave away your fever a bit.

SANTOS: I'm okay.

TEDDY: What have you guy been doing. Seen you come in. Anything happening in your end?

JONES: Not paid yet. We're still trying to fix two and two to get it all out. What is happening on your own end?

TEDDY: Everything is moving fast and the bucks are coming, but the cops are always on the watch.

JONES: Hey Teddy, that reminds me. I would like us to have a private chat on a family matter. Please guys, excuse us.

[*And Jones and Teddy go to the far end of the corner alone.*]

TEDDY: Jones, your friend Santos don't belong with us.

JONES: He's a hard fellow to know, but he can do anything, and he always starts off slow and smooth.

TEDDY: I've got some jobs for you next week. I'm going to pay you quite fine. Here is my mobile number. Give me a call and we will set a time, but it's risky.

JONES: Look, they call me Mr. Risky.

TEDDY: That's my guy, and your cool guy. Santos, bring him along if you think he's okay, and give him the details.

[*Back at the table.*]

SANTOS: Jones we should be leaving. It's late.

JONES: Okay, but wait until I've had my glass of whiskey. I need it to forget so many things and to remember what lies ahead. I know you're not okay with drinking now, but let me have a little myself.

TEDDY: Jones, you still smoke your usual.

JONES: Yes, but I have not seen where to get any.

TEDDY: Let's go over to my car and let me see if I've got any for you.

JONES: Santos, please, just a minute longer.

[*They arrived at the spot where the car was parked.*]

TEDDY: Jones here it is. You can have it all. I will be leaving tomorrow morning for the other side of the island to meet my business partner. You can call me any time. Here is my mobile number. Smoke up, and let me call a cab to take you and Santos home.

[*He calls the taxi and asks Jones to finish up. He says that the cab will be here in ten minutes.*]

JONES: Teddy boy, it's great meeting you.

TEDDY: Jones, you're my guy any time. I still remember those days when we used to go to the seaside to swim together back home, and I'll tease you about that when we get rich I'll marry your kid sister.

JONES: Those were good old days. My sister is now somewhere in America. Why don't we go back to the table while we wait?

[*When they are just about to sit down, the cab arrives. Teddy goes to the driver, speaks to him in the island dialect, and pays him for the trip.*]

SANTOS: Teddy, thanks for everything and also your friends.

TEDDY: It's my pleasure to entertain you because you are my friend. Jones is my main guy.

JONES: Teddy, I'll give you a call tomorrow.

TEDDY: That will be nice.

[*In the car.*]

SANTOS: Look, I don't like to stay out late or to go against the rule of the house.

JONES: It's okay. I'll talk to the chef and tell him it's my fault.

SANTOS: But it's not good to go against laid down rules.

JONES: Are you an advocate for the system? Look, think of better things, how to make money. Look at those guys? They are doing fine not following the rules. I'll explain to the chef.

[*After much explanation and a warning from the chef, they are allowed into the house and told not to come in late again.*]

SANTOS: Look Jones, it's better to always follow rules rather than to be in trouble all of the time.

JONES: It's over. Let's go to bed.

[*In the morning, Oliveria comes to tell Jones and Santos that there is paper work to do today so they should get prepared.*]

OLIVERIA: Hey guys, get ready. There's work for you. There's a new paper we've got to distribute.

SANTOS: Which area are we working today.

JONES: Look, I'm sick so I can't do that job today, and besides that job is too tedious to be done all of the time. And the pay is always too small. You can't buy a nice shirt with the money.

SANTOS: Look Jones, you like the good things in life, but you don't like to work to get them. You are always looking for the easy way out.

JONES: Teddy, my friend, doesn't do this job and he is living a comfortable life, and with a nice girlfriend.

SANTOS: Oliveria, let's get going. Why argue with him?

[*While they are on the way to the work, Jones comes running up to them.*]

JONES: Hey, let me just go with you, just so I won't be left alone.

SANTOS: Jones, why do you always try to discourage people from doing the thing that is right. Not everybody can do the silly thing and survive.

JONES: Mr. Good Guy. Who said you should do silly things.

OLIVERIA: Look, let's discuss something important. Stop this argument. There's the company van with the papers to be distributed.

JONES: The only reward for this kind of job is hard work, and body pain is all you can buy with it.

SANTOS: There is Mr. White, the agent of the company. I think he has been waiting for us.

MR. WHITE: Here boys, you're late so hurry and get started. The paper is not much today, just 3000 pieces.

OLIVERIA: Mr. White, same spot we distributed last time?

MR. WHITE: Yes.

OLIVERIA: Boys, let's start off.

JONES: Yes. Operation Second Slavery, the only reward of a job like this is hard work.

[*They finish the job in less than four hours time.*]

SANTOS: Look Jones, why do you make that statement: "Operation Second Slavery?" Don't you know Mr. White heard you? The job never ever takes us more time, so what is your worry about.

JONES: About you going to suffer what our forefathers suffered.

[*They finished up the job on time.*]

OLIVERIA: Guys, let's find something to eat.

[*They eat and then go back to the house to have some rest.*]

CHAPTER THREE

[*It's Tuesday, 9 o'clock in the morning, and the guys are all hanging around the house. Jones decides to give Teddy a call and goes to the phone booth. Ringing.*]

JONES: Hello! Is this Teddy?
TEDDY: Yes! It's me. Who is on the line?
JONES: Me, Jones.
TEDDY: Yes, hi Jones. How are things on your end?
JONES: Not bad and how about your friends and your business.
TEDDY: Everybody is quite fine and business is moving as normal.
JONES: Look boy, things are no longer moving on fine for me here, so I just thought I'd call to see what you could suggest.
TEDDY: Come over tomorrow and we will talk it over.
JONES: Okay, I'll meet you at exactly 3 o'clock at McDonalds.

[*Jones goes back to the house to look for something to wear for tomorrow so that at least he will look a bit presentable. Jones is all by himself throughout that day, his mind busy thinking of what lies ahead. He goes to sleep early. The following day, at about 11 o'clock, Santos calls Jones and tells him that he has a new job.*]

SANTOS: Jones, I've got a job. It's just an hour's work and the pay is reasonable. It starts off today. You can come along to lunch and then we will get started together.

JONES: Santos, you think you can just tell me to start at some new job without giving me a day's prior notice. Nevertheless, I am not even going to lunch today, let alone talking to you about that work of yours. I just met a girl, and I'm supposed to meet her by 3 o'clock. I'm so happy I can't eat. Go eat well, so that you can continue your hard time.

SANTOS: I know you'll have an excuse like you always do. What time are you meeting this girl of yours again?

JONES: Look boy, stop timing me, okay? I'm not doing this job, period.

SANTOS: Sorry.

[*Oliveria comes to meet them and Jones greets him and goes away.*]

OLIVERIA: Hi Santos, what's up today?

SANTOS: Hi Oliveria. I hope you'll work with me today.

OLIVERIA: Of course. Yes, I'd love to work, at least to be busy doing something, and what's wrong with Jones. Have you two been arguing again?

SANTOS: Oh no. I just don't understand that boy, always wanting the easy way of life. He said he met a girl and he has an appointment by 3 o'clock, but I think he lied.

OLIVERIA: Oh yesterday I saw him on the phone and he spent a long time there. Maybe he is talking with the girl.

SANTOS: You don't understand. It's okay. That's his business anyway.

[*Back in the house: Jones is pressing the clothes he will wear for the meeting. At exactly 2:30, Jones calls a taxi and goes to McDonalds to wait for Teddy. Teddy arrives at exactly 3 o'clock.*]

JONES: Hi Teddy. How's things.

TEDDY: Fine. Why don't we order some food and wine?

JONES: Okay, but you know things have been quite difficult for me.

TEDDY: Don't worry. I'll put you through to another life, put you through my line of business, but all is not that easy – you will have to keep from getting caught by the cops.

JONES: What is the business all about.

TEDDY: We buy wines and leather jackets and smuggle it all over to the other island to sell. It is against the law, but the penalty is just a fine if you get caught, and maybe you'll not even be seen if you're lucky.

JONES: Is that all? Remember that I am Mr. Lucky. I can't even be seen.

TEDDY: The rest you'll learn as you progress in the business. Keeping secrets is more important than what you are used to, okay.

JONES: Okay, that is not a problem. When do I start?

TEDDY: You call me and I'll ask you to come in three days time. How's your guy Santos.

JONES: He is fine. He has got a new girlfriend.

TEDDY: That means he is cool and sharp?

JONES: Yes, he is cool like you said.

TEDDY: Look, I want to take you to my place here in town, so that you can put up there when am not around.

[*He takes Jones to his apartment. Jones exclaims loudly because of what he sees in the apartment, a style of living he has never witnessed before.*]

TEDDY: When I ask you to come, you can come and wait here. Here is the key to the door. I'll pick you up here so that we can cross to the other island.

JONES: Thanks Teddy. You're such a nice fellow. Not many would show another the way to success.

TEDDY: Don't mention it. What are friends for?

[*Jones goes home late again and is cautioned by the chef, and as usual he lies again. Jones goes up to his room and sleeps like the others. The following morning, all get up and as usual the chef has to wake Jones up. After breakfast.*]

SANTOS [*comes over to Jones and talks to him about a job to do today*]: Hi boy. How was your date?

JONES: Not bad at all. That girl is such a beauty. She gave me a nice time, a time never to forget.

SANTOS: I have a job we can both do.

JONES: Look. I'm tired. I need to rest at least today, but okay I'll go with you only because we are friends, not because of the job.

[They arrive at the site of the job and, as usual, Jones keeps murmuring and complaining, always wanting the easy way of life. They finish the job in about two hours.]

SANTOS: Thanks Jones. I'll balance you when I get the pay. When you actually apply yourself and work, you do a good job.

JONES: Look, don't give me that slavery praise, okay? You're my friend, and I can't hide things from you. It wasn't any girlfriend I went to see yesterday. It was Teddy I had an appointment with.

SANTOS: How is he?

JONES: He's fine. He extends greetings to you. He told me all about his business and promised to put me through. He says they buy wine and leather jackets and smuggle it all to the next island to sell for a good profit.

Santos: Is he registered as a company? If his not then it's against the law.

JONES: Look, the penalty is fine of USD $2000.

SANTOS: Just count me out of this okay.

JONES: And again he is organising boys for a football manager who picks them up to play on contract for some club.

SANTOS: Why not tell him we play football?

JONES: Why do think I'm so happy? I already told him and there and then he called the manager and told him about us. I'll be meeting him again in two days time, and I can tell you then when we will be going to see the manager and probably train with a club for an assessment.

SANTOS: That's fine! I think I had better train hard. Can we take Oliveria along too?

JONES: Look, later he can be introduced. Let's don't rush things, okay?

[In two days time Jones goes to the apartment and waits for Teddy. He is trying to figure out how to get Santos into the business without letting Santos know what he is really doing until he gets involved and later decides to join because of the pay involved. Two hours later, Teddy arrives and together they drive to the storehouse beside the lake where six men are waiting, two in the boat the rest in the storehouse loading the goods.]

TEDDY: Look Jones, this is the job. You got to be fast. Everything has to be finished according to exact calculations. Timing is everything. The goods arrive here at about 5 o'clock and at exactly 6:15 they must be on the other side of the island. This "time factor" allows us to just beat the security. Now you can join the others. For each day's work, you get USD $300 to start.

JONES [*works that day and collects his pay. He goes home, bringing some nice things he bought for himself and Santos*]: Hi Santos. This for you I bought it. The manager gave me some little amount in advance for my expenses. I told him I'd bring you along next week.

SANTOS: Thanks boy. I've really trained hard for football.

[Jones has been doing the job for one week and

now he looks obviously different from the other guys of the house. The chef notices the changes in him and asks him about it, but as usual he lies. He says he has got a girlfriend who happens to be the daughter of the football manager. Back at Jones new job, Teddy has now changed his duties. All he does is stay with Teddy as a contact man at a cafe bar. Teddy's driver picks up some things, drops off the other suitcase, and Jones' job was to always be with the merchandise. After three days in the new arrangement, he decides to bring Santos so that he will have company when with the contact person, but he chooses to lie to Santos that this person is the football manager's assistant. The appointment time is usually 4:25 and they must stay until 5:45 when the driver comes. On getting home that day, Jones calls Santos.]

JONES: Santos, tomorrow we will be going to see the manager, but you are not to ask the manager questions about football because he has already made his decision. So he won't think you are just anther hungry guy trying to make it in football.

SANTOS: Okay, if it's okay by you.

[They all eat and go to sleep.]

CHAPTER FOUR

[After going to the café bar the first time with Jones and not saying a word to the football manager, Santos decides to speak up and to settle his anxiety about playing football.]

SANTOS: Jones, I've got to speak to this manager next time we come here. Look, how can I just sit like a lump, and moreover nothing about football or me was mentioned all through the day.

JONES: Look Santos, I told you from the very first time, let me do this thing my way. To play football in a foreign country doesn't come that easy, and I've told him about you so why all the worry about having to talk to him again?

SANTOS: What I am talking about is clear. Football is not something that is always talked about, but once it's part of your everyday life, when you are involved either in playing on the field or managing a football club, or even if you are just a writer about football, you can't sit without discussing about the game.

JONES: I don't want another of your arguments today.

[Upon returning from the meeting, Santos decides to go to the evening church service to pray. Santos gets to the church and prays like the others. After prayers, he decides to take a walk around the church. There he meets a girl named Kathy.

She is a pretty young lawyer and a native of Cayman.]

SANTOS: Hi. How are you?

KATHY: Fine.

SANTOS: My name is Santos, and yours?

KATHY: Kathy is the name.

SANTOS: Mrs. or Miss?

KATHY: Miss. I am just 20 years old, and I just finished law school and am practising now, and what do you do?

SANTOS: I'm a victim of political circumstance. I'm here as a political refugee. I work with a paper distribution company, and meanwhile I'm trying to see if I can play football here.

KATHY: How long have you been around.

SANTOS: About seven months now.

KATHY: Have you tried to make contact with some football clubs.

SANTOS: Yes. One I think am supposed to be training with through the contact of my friend, anyway. I was there today, and they never spoke anything about me, not even football, and that is bothering me a lot because I don't know what my friend Jones, who is always playing pranks, is up to. I just don't want to be involved in any dirty deals.

KATHY: How many times have you met this contact person?

SANTOS: Just today.

KATHY: And nothing about football or you as a player was talked about?

SANTOS: Nothing at all.

KATHY: And your friend asked you before going not to talk to the contact person about yourself?

SANTOS: Yes, he said not to and also that I shouldn't bring up any football issue.

KATHY: When are you supposed to meet again?

SANTOS: Tomorrow.

KATHY: Okay, when you meet tomorrow, always try to bring up the issue of football, then whatever happens let me know. I'll be here again in three days time, but you can have my card æ on the back is my home phone number and address. Call when you feel like. And where do you stay?

SANTOS: House '7' on 2nd Avenue.

KATHY: You mind if I drop you there with my car?

SANTOS: Thanks a lot, and God bless you.

KATHY: How often do you come to church?

SANTOS: Every Sunday and for evening service twice a week. And you?

KATHY: I started last month. It's just two months since my return from America where I was studying.

SANTOS: You were in America? How's it there?

KATHY: Not bad at all.

SANTOS: Stop. I will get out here. That is house seven over there.

KATHY: Okay. Good-bye and good luck. Phone if the need arises, okay?

SANTOS: Okay, I'll phone you tomorrow evening after my meeting.

KATHY: That will be nice.

SANTOS: Thanks for all. Bye.

[Santos is a bit late to the house and is cautioned and his transgression written in the book by the chef Mr. Dandy. The following day he goes to the same spot with Jones, but this time he decides to ask questions.]

SANTOS: Jones, you know I don't know the manager's name.

MR. EDWARD: My name is Edward.

SANTOS: Oh Mr. Edward, how did you find the last world-cup in America.

MR. EDWARD: Which world-cup?

SANTOS: The last Fifa football world-cup won by Brazil.

MR. EDWARD: Football is not my sport at all.

JONES: Only managing. [*And he laughs trying to change the topic.*]

SANTOS: But as a manager Mr. Edward, certainly you like the game.

JONES: He likes the game of managing the money for the people that love the game. Look here comes the driver.

MR. EDWARD: Right on time. I must get going to catch my flight.

SANTOS: You came by plane?

MR. EDWARD: Always, to save time, and its security proof.

[The driver comes to the table and drops the suitcase, then he picks up the other in a clever way, as if this were his bag all along. Suddenly, two plainclothes policemen, who have been sitting at the far table, jump up and come straight at them. They pull out guns and ask them to get up. The manager pushes one of the policemen and runs. Unknown to him, the lady at the bar is also a cop, and she pulls out her gun and orders him to wait. He runs past the door, and she tries to jump over the bar and go after him, but he is waiting with a gun in his hand and shoots her once in the head. She dies instantly. But another policeman in a car nearby shoots a series of bullets into the manager, and he falls and dies instantly too. The other three are arrested æ Jones, Santos, and the driver.]

The police: You're all under arrest!

SANTOS: Jones, what is going on here? Somebody explain.

JONES: Ask them.

The police: Don't try any tricks or funny moves. The whole place is full of policemen.

[They were handcuffed and taken to the station, where they were all kept in different cells.

Back at the house, Mr. Dandy is worried because the two boys have not come back. He decides to call up the police in the morning if they are yet in the house. But that morning, there is news on the national radio station that the police have broken a ring of the most wanted Mafia drug lord in the country and that many people at the scene of the incident were being held for questioning. On a hunch, Mr. Dandy goes to the station to see if Jones and Santos were among those being held for questioning. The police tell him that they are the main dealers or top men in the Mafia ring. Mr. Dandy is shocked, and the police ask him a series of questions about the two boys. He tells the police that they are always coming into the house late and always looking drunk, especially Jones.

The police advises Mr. Dandy not to get a lawyer for the boys as this involves criminal charges and the police will not be happy if the 'house' is in support of such acts. Mr. Dandy tells them it is a rule of the house not to get involved in criminal matters.

That morning the incident is the headline of all the national dailies. Kathy is shocked at what she reads because she knows quite well, in her heart, that Santos is innocent. Or perhaps this isn't even the same man.]

CHAPTER FIVE

[The Cayman news radio and television stations have been talking of the current arrest by the police. Kathy reads about it in one of the national dailies also, but she isn't sure if the man she met on the church premises is the person involved. However, the story she reads in the dailies about the boy give his statement, which matches closely what she discuss with the boy, and 'Kathy,' her name, was mentioned once by the boy. She speaks with her father about the issue, but he says she should forget it, that his years and wealth of experience regarding such cases have made him not believe any criminal. It certainly sounds like Santos, so Kathy decides to check the police station where the boys are been held to be certain.]

KATHY: Officer, I'm here to visit Santos Pedro.

OFFICER: Are you related to him?

KATHY: No, I'm a lawyer and I met him some time ago before the arrest I am the Kathy he mentions in his statement, the person he says he met at the church.

OFFICER: Can I see an identity card, driver's licence, or passport.

KATHY: Here is my passport.

OFFICER: Fill out the visitor form please.

KATHY: Thanks.

OFFICER: Come with me. I will take you to the visitors' room where you will meet him.

[And she was taken to the room. She waited and Santos was called to meet her.]

KATHY: Hi Santos. How do you feel? I hope all is okay with you, as okay as you can be under these circumstances.

SANTOS: I'm okay, but I don't know how to explain myself. I'm in a confused world, dreaming maybe, and I hope it will come to an end soon.

KATHY: Take it easy. Just tell me how it happened. I know you're innocent.

SANTOS: Before I could ask the so-called manager about football, the police pounced on us, and there was a shoot out as the manager was about to escape. The police found drugs in the briefcase that was on the side of the table, and now they are charging me along with the others for dealing drugs and possession of firearm. I feel like dying.

KATHY: It's okay. I'll do my best to see that you're not found guilty of this shit, because I know and believe you are innocent. Did they give you a lawyer?

SANTOS: Yes.

KATHY: Have you met him?

SANTOS: Yes. Here his card. He dropped it and asked me to call him when I am ready to tell him the truth. He doesn't believe my story, and he's advising me to plead guilty, saying it will reduce my sentence.

KATHY: Look, never plead guilty, because you're innocent and I know that. Meanwhile, can I have the lawyer's card? I'd like to speak to him. I'm taking up the case myself.

SANTOS: But I've got no money to pay you.

KATHY: I'm doing it for free.

SANTOS: Thanks. God bless you.

KATHY: If you need any material thing, call on me,

and I'll also drop some money with the police in case you need to buy some things.

SANTOS: I'm so grateful.

[She says goodbye and leaves. Santos is taken back to his cell in the yard. Kathy is very sad when she arrives home, and her father tries to ask what the matter is but she doesn't want to discuss it with anybody. After much pleading, she decides to tell her father the problem.]

KATHY: Daddy the problem is I know that boy Santos is innocent of all charges.

DADDY: I think you should forget about that boy's case, because knowing someone for just one day can't give you a proper assessment of their character or their motives.

KATHY: The circumstance present at a point in time always lead one to believe things in a particular order.

DADDY: Don't let sentimental reason ruin your sense of reason, or your sense of who deserves your attention and who does not.

KATHY: You just don't like him because he is a foreigner in our land. Nevertheless, I don't want to bring up this issue. I think I better fight this case alone.

DADDY: Look, forget about that boy and that case in order to protect your name. Don't you know the press and media will all have their eyes on you until and after the case?

Mum: Kathy, I think you should listen to your father. He has a point, but I know you feel for that boy.

KATHY: I've said I'm fighting this war alone, my name and your pride I've got to put behind to help an innocent victim. Circumstances have put us into thinking negatively of this situation.

MUM: Why are you so concerned about this boy anyway, or is there something between you.

KATHY: Mum, I think that's my life and my business.

MUM: I know it's your life and your business, but you know that you are our only child and we love you and won't let you get involved in something that will weigh you down. You should know that your father and I love you enough to intervene.

KATHY: If you love me, then respect my feelings.

MUM: Okay, we will think about it.

[Kathy nevertheless continues to visit Santos. On one of her visits, Santos tells her that only seeing her makes him feel relieved and happy, that he is planning to write a book and would like her to assist him in its publication. He tells her that sometimes everything seems lost to him, but writing is the only thing that can be done now that he is in prison and he needs her encouragement. She promises to assist him up until the time he gets a fair judgement and is set free.

The last hearing of the case comes up in two days time and she comes around with her friend, who is also a lawyer, to ask Santos some questions and to advise him on how best to answer matters while in the court. Oliveria also came with them. The name of Kathy's co-lawyer and friend is Jean Brown.]

KATHY: Santos, just answer the questions with ease and tell the whole episode that happened, starting from the first day Jones took you to meet his friend Teddy at McDonalds and ending with the so-called manager issue and your subsequent arrest. We will be right behind you to counter any irrelevant questions. Just try not to panic.

JEAN: Just take things easy. Your friend Oliveria will be in the courtroom also. So don't feel that the world is against you. We're right behind you.

SANTOS [*crying*]: How do I thank you for all these things you're doing for me, most especially you Kathy. If not for you, how would I fight this judgmental war of circumstance alone?

JEAN: I know you're just a victim of circumstance, and justice must be done to see that you are released.

KATHY: Oliveria is outside in the yard. The police wouldn't allow more than two of us in to visit you, so he dropped you this note.

Santos: Tell him I am more than happy for him to come to visit me, and ask him if he still plays football.

KATHY: Oh yes, but not often of late, as he is always thinking of you.

[A policeman comes to tell the two ladies that the time for visiting is over, that the boy must go back into his cell. Kathy says good-bye to Santos and tells him that she brought him some food and that the police will give it to him after they search the container. Santos thanks her and is taken back to his room. Kathy and Jean go home to prepare their case for the coming trial in two days time. Oliveria is to visit them in Jean's office tomorrow, and then they will go to a coffee shop to talk over the case.

Oliveria comes to Jean's office and finds her trying to clean up Coca-Cola, which has just poured over the table. He helps her clean it up. She is surprised and very happy because a man in Cayman Islands will rarely do such a thing, as they are such proud people.]

JEAN: Thanks Oliveria. I think Kathy should be here in the next ten minutes. She just called me before you arrived.

OLIVERIA: Look, I don't know how to thank you and

Kathy for the help you are giving to my friend Santos.

JEAN: Kathy so likes that boy Santos now that she will do anything for his release, and I also like the boy. I respect Kathy feelings because we have been friends from youth and we both went to the states together to study law.

OLIVERIA: How was it in America?

JEAN: Quite fine and the people there are better off than we are down here. There is a lot of opportunity. Most especially for those in both the entertainment field and sports.

[Then there is a knock on the door and Kathy enters the office, greets the others, and they all go to the coffee bar. They talk things over for three hours and then all go home. Jean drops Oliveria at the house with her car.

The next day the court session starts at ten o'clock in the morning. The court clerk reads the charges in the case and names the defendants. The prosecutor for the police speaks quite well and very cleverly implicates all those arrested in the incident, obviously making sure that all the boys were charged equally and with no exceptions.

Kathy defends the boy and tries to explain to the judge that he's just a victim of circumstance. She tries to tell the court that anger and rate of crime should not be the basis for judgement, but instead they should look into the financial affairs of the boys, that this boy Santos has nothing at all that is material in his life.

The judge says that if her client is to be proven innocent, that it will not be her argument or herself as a witness that will accomplish that. The boys caught with Santos are the only people who can prove his innocence. He passes the sentence and all defendants get eight-year jail terms. Kathy cries and promises Santos that she's going to fight for a retrial.

Throughout the trial, the occupants of 'house 7' refuse to come to see the boys and this the prosecutor uses against them, telling the court that the boys have such a bad record with the house their fellows refuse to come to the boys aid.]

CHAPTER SIX

[As Santos and Jones get their sentence of eight years each, Teddy receives ten years as well. They are all being kept in the same prison, and there they now have the chance to see and talk to one another. Meanwhile, Santos continues to write his book, hoping when he finishes that Kathy will help him get it published. Jones has been attending the bible meeting of a fellowship group that visits the prison twice a week. Teddy is now practising boxing in prison.

It has been one year now, and the date of a retrial of the case has been fixed. It comes up in three months time. Kathy comes to visit Santos every week in prison. On one of her visits she tells Santos to plead with Jones, that only Jones' testimony that he knows little or nothing about the offence could set him free. The following day during the normal hour at the prison for walking about the prison grounds, Santos decides to talk to Jones about it.]

SANTOS: Jones, I would like to talk to you for a minute.
Jones: Oh? What about?
SANTOS: About me and you, about my condition.
Jones: Oh, I know the prison is affecting you. Eight years is too long to imagine being in such a place, but I think in the next four months the foreign police department will come to send us home. I heard that the rule here on Cayman is when the court gives a person eight years and he or she is a foreigner he serves just sixteen months and is

then taken to his or her country. So have no fear. We will be home in three months time.

SANTOS: Look Jones, you know I didn't have anything to do with this crime am just a victim of circumstance, and you're the only one who can set me free.

Jones: Why should I go back to the police and tell another story now when I know that we will be going home in three months time, and meanwhile Teddy promises to give us much financial assistance back home? So why the worry, after all they wouldn't allow us to stay on Cayman any longer?

SANTOS: Look, Kathy has already succeeded in appealing for retrial of the case, and the date has been fixed. It comes up next three months.

Jones: Look, I don't know what you are up to? Do you want them to increase my jail term and set you free? And why are you bringing out tears from your eyes? Just give me a few days to think it over.

SANTOS: Thanks Jones. Please, if you do it, I'll never forget you, and God will continue to bless you.

Jones: I'll give you an answer when I see you tomorrow.

[The next day Jones meets Santos and says he has decided to tell the court the true story. He has also told the church members the truth and they have promised to get him a lawyer during the possible retrial and also to prepare a visa for him to go to Canada to study theology.

Meanwhile, Kathy plans to marry Santos in prison so that the foreign police won't take him home immediately after the court frees him. They get married two weeks before the retrial of the case. The Cayman media and television station carry the news of the marriage and the retrial of the case throughout that month. One of the captions in the dailies reads: Prison of Conscience, and Love has no Bounds. The television reporter says, "Love is stronger than pride."

Oliveria has since gotten married to Kathy's friend and his doing fine working with a tourist company, and Kathy's mother has joined Kathy in her struggle to see that Santos becomes a free person. Her father is also contributing a little advice to his daughter on how to tackle the case in court. He gives her all his old cases that are related to the present one.

It is just three days to the day of the retrial of the case. Santos' book has already been published and it will be launched a day before the retrial. The publisher of the book says that the book is going to generate a lot of attention from the public and he is going to make the name Santos Pedro a very popular name in the publishing world. Kathy comes to see Santos after the launching of the book to have a final chat with him before the court session the next day.]

KATHY: Hello Santos. How do you feel today?

SANTOS: Fine, just a bit worried about tomorrow. Meanwhile, how are you and the family? You've been working too hard. Just don't get run down.

KATHY: I'm okay. I can't get run down because I must continue to fight to see that my husband is released.

SANTOS: Every day I sit here and think of you, and the more I think, the more I love you.

KATHY: Just take it easy. I love you too and I also think of your immediate release so that we can start a future together.

SANTOS: I have spoken to Jones, and he still agrees to tell the court the whole truth about my side in the incident. His fellowship group plans to fly him to Canada to study theology.

KATHY: That will be very nice. Then your chances of acquittal are bright now. And my father, after failing to stop the marriage and knowing full well that if he doesn't stop being against you I'll have to change my family name, is finally accepting this marriage and will help me with your case. Last night my mother came over to my new apartment to tell me that my father is sick and he's at the hospital, so I rushed to see him. He apologised for his being negative about my feelings toward you and promises to help me with advice on the case.

SANTOS: Oh I'm so happy, but why should I cause you and your family such problems.

KATHY: Now you are my husband, so I'm not doing things for you as a friend or some outsider but as my better half. Your book was launched today, and the launching was great. The publisher says the book is going to make lots of money for you.

SANTOS: Thanks for everything.

KATHY: I'll be going to get prepared for the case tomorrow. I pray you will be released tomorrow.

SANTOS: I hope and pray too.

KATHY: Oliveria and Jean will be at the trial tomorrow, and so will my mother. I'll go now dear, bye.

SANTOS: Bye dear. See you tomorrow.

[At the court the next day: Jones stands up and tells the court that he got Santos involved in all this, and that Santos knows nothing about the incident, that he's just a victim of circumstance. Jones pleads guilty and confesses to the court that all this happened just because he failed to be contented with what he has, but now he knows that crime doesn't pay and money is not everything.

The court, after hearing this, frees Santos and reduces Jones sentence to two years or fine of $20,000. The fellowship ministry pays the fine and

Jones was set free and taken to Canada to study theology.

Santos now lives with Kathy and has become a very popular writer.

Oliveria now operates his own business. He's doing fine as well.]

INSTIGATOR

A Play

CHAPTER ONE

[Inside the office sit Johnny and Brandon. They've been together in the same office for 3 years, but Johnny happens to have been in that office longer by one year, and he has also been with the company 3 years longer than Brandon. On this Monday morning, Johnny and Brandon are together in the office and discussing their employer.]

Johnny: Brandon, you now what baffles me about this company. I don't understand why some people must work so hard and others don't, and just because of a man's educational qualifications, he can work very little but get more money and get quicker promotions. Look at old so-and-so, for instance. I've been here longer than he has, and yet he has control over me, how I do my work and even what work I do. But guys like him with their education still don't know the job so well as I do, and I, Johnny, must always explain the job to them. And you know what annoys me most? They make so much noise and feel so superior and are always very indignant when speaking to one of us. They're always waiting for you to greet them first, even when they see you before you see them.

I'm so happy for this degree that you're achieved through you part-time courses. I know by next year you'll be moving to the office upstairs to sit with those who think they are more important than we are. All I know is that you won't turn up your nose when you see me like those others up there.

BRANDON: Johnny, after 3 years together, I'm happy

you know me so well, and I'm also happy to have learned a lot from you. My moving up to that office will never change who I am or my relationship with you. I've been so close to you, both at work and outside work. We are the best friends and my family all know you so well. I will ways be grateful to you. You know it was your idea that I embark on this degree course, and I never can forget that, or how you helped me and encouraged me all along the way. I can't thank you enough.

JOHNNY: I'm happy for you Brandon. Really, you don't know how happy I am. You see, you are like a brother to me. You know what I like most about you? It's your show of appreciation for all that I did for you, because I know so many I've helped in life that don't even show a little sign of appreciation. Even in this very office, as you have witnessed, those who come and I show them everything and give them my advice, but today they hardly answer me when I greet them, to mention nothing of greeting me first.

BRANDON: Never mind those ridiculous people. I know what you've done for them, most especially Mr. Felix, but today you see how he behaves, and that girl. I was about to ask the secretary to the director, Vivian, on a date, and you can see how he shouldered me away and got to her through the influence of his position.

JOHNNY: Just don't worry Brandon you'll get Vivian, and any of the other girls in the office if you like. I will work out a plan for you.

BRANDON: I don't want the other girls. It's Vivian I like. Look, there is something special in that girl that I like so much. And what is the plan you've got because I know you really know how to work things out.

JOHNNY: You know that girls like people with position and prestige, so I advise you to do more professional course work so that you can get higher than Felix in the company. And the rest of plan will work out the details.

BRANDON: The next degree to get me up into a higher position will definitely take a minimum six month program of intensive courses with intensive reading day and night. You know that is not easy.

JOHNNY: You said so before the last course, but at last you come out the best in the class. I know you can make it again. Just do this course and Vivian is yours for the asking.

BRANDON: Give me a few days to give it some thought.

JOHNNY: It's getting close to lunchtime. Have you finished programming those new designs into the computer?

BRANDON: Yes I have.

JOHNNY: Come on then, let's go get some lunch, and we can have a glimpse of those beautiful girls.

BRANDON: Johnny, its 20min before 12 noon. You know how the personnel director hates it when we leave early. If we go sit in the café room before the proper time…well, I don't want anyone to insult me today.

JOHNNY: Fuck that director. I've been in this organisation 2 years longer than he has. Come on, let's go. Sooner or later you will be in his position, or even higher up the corporate ladder than him.

BRANDON: If you insist, Johnny. Okay, we'll go. Just let me shut down my computer.

[Johnny and Brandon walk though the passage to the café dining room, and on their way they meet Susan, a close friend of Vivian's.]

SUSAN: Hi Johnny. Hi Brandon.

[Johnny and Brandon say hi to Susan at the same time.]

JOHNNY: Susan, I cant hide telling you how beautiful you look in that red dress of yours, and you know what? Red is my favourite.

SUSAN: Thank you, Johnny. Red happens to be my favourite as well.

BRANDON: Susan, how is your friend Vivian?

SUSAN: Brandon, you never forget to ask about this Vivian girl every time you see me.

JOHNNY: Its like if one wants to know much about a city he wants to visit or live in he needs a city guide or someone who at least knows the city very well.

SUSAN: This is what I admire about you, the way you resolve matters. But oh poor Brandon, I can imagine how you feel.

JOHNNY: Oh it's noon Susan. Are you going to the café or do you have something to talk about with those guys above us.

SUSAN: I have nothing to talk with anyone about. Let's get something to drink in café, we three.

[They go to the café dining room together, and Johnny gets Susan a cup of coffee and Brandon a cup of tea.]

SUSAN: Thanks Johnny. How do you know I drink black coffee?

JOHNNY: I guess I've been watching over your shoulder for so long.

BRANDON: Johnny, what guys were you referring to that Susan is always having discussions with.

JOHNNY: Those in the executive class, whom you will soon be joining up there.

SUSAN: Oh Brandon, don't tell me you have passed the degree course.

BRANDON: Yes I have.

SUSAN: We've got to celebrate.

JOHNNY: Of course we will celebrate! In fact, I have planned a party for him at my place on Saturday, and I hope you will come and that you will bring Vivian with you.

SUSAN: Of course I'll come, and I hope Vivian will have time too. Oh, here comes Vivian now. Hello Vivian. Sit over here with us. There is a free place for you.

SUSAN [*bends and whispers to Brandon*]: I know you like it when she sits next to you for a cup of coffee.

VIVIAN: Hi Susan. Hi Brandon and hi Johnny.

BRANDON: Hi Vivian.

Johnny: Hi Vivian, but why must I be greeted last?

VIVIAN: Oh Johnny, you always have something to complain about.

JOHNNY: Vivian would like fruit-tea I presume. [*He stands up to get her the tea.*]

VIVIAN: How do you know what I like to drink?

SUSAN: He seems to be watching over the two of us.

JOHNNY: I got the hint about what you like to drink from Brandon. [*Now Johnny is seated with them at the table.*]

VIVIAN: But I didn't hear Brandon say a word to you just now, or was it pre-discussed?

JOHNNY: You should know that when someone cares about someone else they talk about things to do with that someone, even little things. Oh, about the party. Susan, give Vivian the news.

SUSAN: Clever. I see how you changed the topic. Now it's the party. Why don't you just tell her yourself? You mentioned the party to her already.

JOHNNY: It's already been told so she just has to ask me what party I'm talking about.

BRANDON: Johnny, why don't you take a course in politics or law. You've got a clever way of staging your defence in any matter.

VIVIAN: Johnny, one thing about you is that you are very defensive, and have a very convincing voice, and that smile is something else, so no matter what you say its very difficult for one to get angry with you very easily.

SUSAN: Vivian, he is also seductive, so I cant believe him when he says he doesn't have a girlfriend because he can talk any girl he likes into falling for him, and you're right, that smile would just knock anybody off their feet.

JOHNNY: Really, I am free at the moment. I just think I'm too busy or too tired to get into a relationship. I don't want to start a relationship that I can't hold onto for a long time I don't want to be a heartbreaker, or let someone break mine for that matter. I want something that will last forever. I mean… Oh, here comes Mr Felix. Hi Felix.

FELIX: Hi Vivian. Hi Susan. [*He just raises up a finger as a gesture to Johnny and Brandon. He takes Vivian's hand and pulls her up gently then escorts her to a table at the far end of the café.*]

SUSAN: I hate this Felix. He is the kind of guy who feels so superior. Look at the way he greeted you two and then he just took Vivian away from us here without a word. Look, he could just pull up a chair and sit with us at this table. There is enough space here.

BRANDON: Susan, don't let it disturb you. Maybe he has something private or special to discuss with Vivian.

SUSAN: Brandon, you're just a perfect gentleman. You are inarguably the right guy for Vivian, not that arrogant thing.

JOHNNY: There is nothing private in their discussion. He's just trying to degrade us.

SUSAN: Oh, time is up. I must get back to my work. I've got a lot on my desk today.

JOHNNY: Susan, have you got anything on your desk about the Olympic Stadium project?

SUSAN: I saw it this morning, but I've not really gone through it. See you guys tomorrow or after work, and I can't stop thinking about the party. Oh I love dancing, ooh la, la, la.

JOHNNY: The way you move that ass… oh, I mean that waist of yours is some thing else.

[And they stand up to go back to their offices.]

SUSAN: Johnny, you better not be calling my waist my ass. [*She laughs as she walks away with a more sexually provocative step, swinging her hips.*]

BRANDON: Johnny, that girl's waist is something else and the way she just moved is applaudable. But women, what's the difference between complimenting her waist and her ass.

JOHNNY: Waist is respectable, while ass is associated with asshole or commercialised, prostituted even. You see, these days women want to be respected and don't want themselves to seen as a tool used in the satisfaction of our sexual urges.

[Johnny and Brandon walk back into their office].

BRANDON: Johnny, do you still think I've got a chance to get to this Vivian. I think she's falling head-over-heels in love with this Felix.

JOHNNY: Love? She has just fallen for his position not his person. Look, you think she would just fall for him if he happened to be in the same position as we are? Never. Just watch and see how she will start coming to you when you get up to that higher post. She will make a U-turn in a one way drive.

BRANDON: I hope so because I like that woman a lot. And what about you? Don't you want to achieve a better position, or are you content to remain in this position?

JOHNNY: I will think of something later, but right now I'm more focused on my joint venture with my brother.

BRANDON: For so long I've forgotten to ask you, but how is the joint venture with your brother moving. I know you told me you want no one in our organisation to know about it, so I have refrained from asking you about it often.

JOHNNY: It is coming along gradually, but it's coming fine. We just got a contract to paint the newly built shopping complex at 4th Avenue.

BRANDON: You don't say. Such a big shopping complex means you are in the money now.

JOHNNY: Not so much as you might think. But please, I don't want anyone here to know about it or to know about my brother. You know Brandon, since I left my ex-girl friend, May Brown, I have found it difficult to fall for anyone again... but this girl Susan.

BRANDON: What about her? Don't tell me you are crazy about her.

JOHNNY: Well maybe I just like her as a person, nothing more.

BRANDON: She's a pretty and intelligent girl and would be a perfect match for you.

JOHNNY: I know she's got quality, but right now I don't want to get into a relationship. Oh, but that ass of hers... I mean that waist of hers, just seems to be driving me wild.

BRANDON: Oh, you just want to have a shot at that. [*And he laughs.*]

JOHNNY: I don't think she's that silly to fall for a quick one. And you, I know you really want to have someone for the keeping, someone like Vivian.

BRANDON: She's my dream come true.

JOHNNY: Brandon, when will you be submitting your credentials to the director. You know it's better if you submit them now so that you can be quickly considered for post elevation.

BRANDON: Don't you think it would be better to wait

until I finish the next degree course work so that I can submit it all at the same time? It would enhance my chances even more.

JOHNNY: I like your strategy, but I still think it would be better if you elevate gradually as this will improve your on-the-job knowledge. And people will not start speaking about your sudden triple jump. Then when you achieve the next degree-level you can submit and move forward while you're already up there, and the company will not hesitate to elevate you because you now know the rudiments about the job at all the various stages. Then I will know that my right-hand man is really up there in a high position because he can do the job.

BRANDON: If things work out for me just as you've said, I don't think I can ever forget you, because my achievement is due in large part to your ideas and planning.

JOHNNY: You see Brandon, I have always known you are a different kind of person from every friend I have had in the past, those whom I have helped and those who have help me as well. So I never ever give it a thought that you can suddenly change just because of success.

BRANDON: Success or no success, you help me or I help you, and the Brandon you see today is the same Brandon you will see tomorrow and always, the same person with the same character.

JOHNNY: Brandon, why don't we go for a drink after work at the Wild Hut [*This is a popular joint where the interior is built in an African–Mexican design with flowers and bamboo and a neatly installed waterfall springing out from a rock.*] You know I love that place. That strange motif seems somehow natural and appealing.

BRANDON: That will be nice. Yes, we can go there after work.

[Work ends at 5. p.m., and Brandon and Johnny drive to the Wild Hut. It is situated in the heart of the city. They both drive in their separate cars and arrive at the Wild Hut in 20 minutes.

BRANDON: Johnny, you know why I like it here? It makes you feel relaxed and think you are on a Caribbean Island or in a safari hut somewhere in Africa. Here you forget your problems and think of the happiness of nature and its beauty.

JOHNNY: What would you like to eat or drink? For me, I think I would like pizza and a glass of beer to chase it down.

BRANDON: Id also like pizza but with an orange soft drink mixed with pineapple.

[Johnny calls the waiter over and makes the order.]

JOHNNY: Brandon, you know the company is going to start the design of the ultra-modern Olympic Stadium project next month, and now that our company has bought the Walls construction company, I think the building of the project will be done by Walls. But the painting, I don't know what firm that work will be allocated to but I know it's our firm who decides on what firm must do the painting.

BRANDON: Why don't you make an application now for the painting, your... I mean you and your brother's firm could be approved for the work.

JOHNNY: Ours is such a small firm and new at the same time, and to get such a contract you need connections. You see, once you're up in that position, then I could say at least I have got a 50-50 chance to get the contract.

BRANDON: So it is better if I submit my credentials for the promotion tomorrow.

JOHNNY: That's a step forward, a step in the right direction. Oh, here comes the waiter with our orders. I'm so hungry.

BRANDON: It smells so nice. I love pizza.

[They stay 2 hours eating and drinking.]

[The next day at work, Brandon submits his credentials to the executive board and is very luck because there is a vacant post and the position has something to do with painting design and Brandon happens to hold this qualification. The company accepts his application and he is told he will be moving up to that position in two weeks time. Brandon left the board of directors' office so happy and eager to tell Johnny about his up-coming promotion.]

BRANDON: Johnny, you see God is great. I submitted my credentials at exactly the same time the company is looking for someone with my qualifications.

JOHNNY: Oh, that's great, and what position were you given?

BRANDON: You won't believe it, but it's a new department and it has to do with painting and design.

JOHNNY: I knew that a department like this one would soon be opened here because the company now makes painting decisions before giving out the bid to a painting firm. That's great Brandon, and exactly when will you be moving up?

BRANDON: In two weeks, but I really will miss this office and most importantly you.

JOHNNY: Come on. I'll also miss you, but you're still in the same building with me, and your new office is just two floors above this one.

BRANDON: This really calls for a big celebration.

JOHNNY: For sure. We must celebrate this news, and it will happen this weekend at my place. I have a plan to stage a big surprise party for you.

[The week goes by quickly and it is Friday, the last day of work before the party.]

BRANDON: Johnny, after work we have to hurry to do

some shopping for tomorrow. I think its better if I put up at your place so that we can both prepare the cooking as early as possible.

JOHNNY: Not to worry, my brother, Evans, will do the rest of the shopping. I've already discussed it with him, and about the cooking, Evans' girlfriend and one of her friends are going to do the cooking.

BRANDON: Then give me the bills so that I can pay later.

JOHNNY: Brandon it's a party from both of us, me and my brother, and for you the bill is on us.

BRANDON: I'll never forget you and all you've done for me. I'm ever ready to help you in what ever needs arise in life. Just count on me, Johnny.

[After the work, Brandon prepares some little surprises for the party, and Johnny also rushes home to join his brother in the preparation. At Johnny's place:]

JOHNNY: Evans, thanks for getting everything ready. You've really done a lot of shopping.

EVANS: It all went so easy and fast with Irene here all day to help.

JOHNNY: This girlfriend of yours is always ready to help. I presume she skipped the lecture at the university today.

EVANS: She bought everything here with her own cash.

JOHNNY: That's what is good in having a girl with wealthy parents. They always have a lot to spend for those who know the use of money. She really wants to be in the house.

EVANS: I know she's not that pretty, but her cash works magic. Johnny, it was your idea and your plan that got her for me.

JOHNNY: She's really paying the bill for having a very handsome man, and her connection to her father was why we got the shopping complex project.

EVANS: Johnny, are you sure after we do all this for Brandon that he won't refuse to approve the painting of the Olympic project for us.

JOHNNY: Brother, never worry. His mind is made up to do anything for us, Just watch and see how our firm, Jovans Group, is going to expand to be a very big firm in the future.

EVANS: You mean we will get the contract to paint the new Olympic Stadium complex.

JOHNNY: It's an 85% chance, I think. I'm working everything I can think of to improve the odds as much as possible. Oh Evans, I hope your girlfriend is bring her friend Pat to help her tomorrow with the cooking.

EVANS: Yes, Patty is coming along, but I think Patty is still mad at you for the way you used her and dumped her. I think she wanted more than that from you, I mean a relationship.

JOHNNY: What will I do with her? She is so empty, no money, no rich connection. Right now I'm aiming at the top. I don't want this kind of person now. I need one with money and contacts all over.

EVANS: What about Vivian? I think you like her because of the way you speak when you talk about her.

JOHNNY: I'll get her when the time is ripe, but right now I must work her out for Brandon so that he can be happy. You know a happy man does all that is asked of him, but right now I'll stick to Susan, Vivian's best friend, so that there will be no distance between me and Vivian and I can closely watch Brandon.

EVANS: I'll watch to see how you will plot out this coup again.

JOHNNY: But never mention anything about my interest on Vivian to your girl Irene.

EVANS: Brother, I know our aim, so my lips are sealed on this issue.

JOHNNY: It's getting late and I'm feeling tired. I think I will go to sleep.

[On Saturday, Johnny and Evans wake up very early to clean the house and prepare the things the girls need for the cooking. Irene and Patty come at 9 o'clock to start the cooking and Brandon comes at 10 o'clock.]

BRANDON: Johnny, oh I think these girls' cooking is excellent. I can smell the aroma of the cooking from outside. I've got a few wines as a surprise in my car. I will bring them in.

JOHNNY: I'll come with you.

EVANS: I'll come too.

BRANDON: It's not so much.

JOHNNY: My God, there is a lot of wine here and you said it isn't much. Who will finish all of this drink, and of course we bought about the same quantity.

EVANS: Brandon, first I must say congratulations on your success, but my brother and I are staging this party on your behalf so you didn't have spend that much. I have got an idea. I think I'll ask my girl to go to her school and bring in some willing girls to come and party with us. After all, we've got more than enough.

JOHNNY: Good idea Evans.

BRANDON: Johnny, I know you like the sight of girls everywhere.

JOHNNY: I'll bet you like it as well.

BRANDON: I like girls, that's a fact, but my mind is focused on Vivian. I still don't know what makes me so crazy about her.

JOHNNY: Vivian is truly a pretty and intelligent girl.

EVANS: I'll go to meet the girls, and I'll try to tell Irene to bring the other girls for the party.

BRANDON: What if Vivian shows up with this Felix of a guy?

JOHNNY: Never mind. I've set up plans to combat any obstacle standing in the way of your chance with Vivian today.

BRANDON: I hope your plan works, but what is your plan?

JOHNNY: Its going to work. You know Felix is the kind of guy who likes seeing pretty girls around him, and we've arranged for so many girls around he wouldn't care much about Vivian. Hey, come on lets go and get the music set ready.

[At 6 o'clock in the evening, the guests begin to arrive. Six girls and three boys come from Irene's school, and Evans' friend Mike comes also with two more girls. Vivian and Felix come at half past six, so also does Susan. Now it's a full house.

[Johnny and Brandon are going around to greet the guests and to introduce themselves to the new faces. Felix and Vivian are now on the dance flour dancing and Evans is the DJ.]

BRANDON: Hi Susan.

Susan: Hi Brandon. Big congrats! Care to dance with me?

BRANDON: Why not?

[Johnny is also on the dance floor, dancing with Irene, he moves close to Felix and Vivian, and immediately he exchanges Irene with Felix for Vivian, who is now dancing with him. He dances a little while with her and asks her to come out and have a chat with him outside.]

JOHNNY: Vivian, you care for a cigarette?

VIVIAN: Yes, thank you. [*Johnny gives her a cigarette and lights it for her.*]

JOHNNY: Vivian, you are really a pretty girl, and an intelligent one too.

VIVIAN: Oh don't knock me off feet with your compliments, but thanks anyway. What do I say about you, a perfect man, well built, with voice and words to get any women off her feet? You're really the kind of man a woman would always like to have.

JOHNNY: Vivian, you are my kind of girl, no doubt about that. I'd give and do anything to get and keep you, but you are already in the hand of another man and yet another one is deeply in love with you.

VIVIAN: In whose hand do you think I am? Felix is just a friend for the asking, and as for the other one who is deeply in love with me, he is really not my kind of guy. He is old fashioned, and Felix is really not my kind of guy either.

JOHNNY: But then why are you with Felix?

VIVIAN: Oh, just an on the job friend.

JOHNNY: You mean he is job protection or security to cover up for coming in late.

VIVIAN [*laughing*]: Since you put it that way, job protection is good, but for me there is nothing happening between me and him. About this interview, what's your aim? I know men and you in particular, and you're up to something. You've heard what you wanted to hear æ my heart is not occupied by anyone yet.

Johnny: I would have love to occupy it but....

VIVIAN: But what?

JOHNNY: My friend Brandon would love to have you, and I would like it so much if you can pretend to accept him so that he can do me a very big favour.

VIVIAN: Brandon? I don't think he has a chance to be with me. And he must learn that even if he loves a woman and has a castle and money, if she doesn't love him, wealth can't buy her love. Money, name, qualifications, and prestige don't buy love either. Love is natural. How you see the beloved and how the beloved sees you and feels must be guided by the rules of nature.

JOHNNY: What of me?

VIVIAN: For you I will do anything. [*They kiss and promise to love one another dearly, but to keep the relationship a secret from Felix, Susan, Brandon, and even Mike.*]

VIVIAN: I will accept Brandon until he does you the favour you will ask of him, and if I may ask, what is the favour you are asking of Brandon?

JOHNNY: Its just for him to give a recommendation for our company so that the firm will award the painting of the Olympic Stadium complex to my company, Jovans, and not just recommend this project but other projects as well. Look, I need this opportunity to make money to set up a good future for us and for our children.

VIVIAN: And how long will all this take, because I can't hide my love for you that long. I want to be the woman with you and you alone and not the woman you use to solve problems.

JOHNNY: Look, I want you just as much as you want me, and I don't want it to take that long, but I don't want to bring up kids to have financial problems just as I have had, and like I have heard that you had in your youth as well. So, it's an opportunity and we have to make the best use of it.

VIVIAN: What of Felix? Do I push him away too?

JOHNNY: Let him remain on the line. We need him and his signature as well, but you've just got to play the lady's game well on both of them. Just kiss Felix as usual but not intimately and no sex, and Brandon, just hold hands æ no kissing or sex. [*They kiss again and go into the party.*]

BRANDON: Johnny, where have you been all this time. I've been looking around for you.

JOHNNY: Oh, I was outside speaking with Vivian.

BRANDON: May I ask what the discussion was.

JOHNNY: About you and how she feels about the fact that you feel and care for her.

BRANDON: And what was her response?

JOHNNY: At first, she didn't want to believe me, because you should have come to tell her this yourself and she thinks you just want to have a quick one on her.

BRANDON: But I've told her how beautiful she is before, and how I admire her qualities.

JOHNNY: In setting up a relationship, ladies need to be told more, how beautiful they look yes, but you must tell them how you will cherish them and take care of that beauty, protect it and honour everything about her.

BRANDON: You mean if I tell her this she will be mine?

JOHNNY: Of course, yes. In fact, I think she digs you too, and your promotion achievement also helped to work some magic.

BRANDON: Do I go right away to her?

JOHNNY: Of course! Just go and ask her for a dance, then take her out to chat with her. I'll keep a watch on Felix and try to distance him from you two.

BRANDON: Thanks Johnny, I better go right away to her.

[Brandon asks Vivian for a dance, they dance a little, and then Brandon asks her to have a chat with him outside.]

BRANDON: Vivian, you know you look so wonderful in this outfit of yours.

VIVIAN: Thanks, you are looking cool in yours as well.

Brandon: Really?

VIVIAN: Yes, of course.

BRANDON: You see, something has always been disturbing my mind.

VIVIAN: What is that? Is it stress from work or about

your new position? Look, I'm really happy for your achievement.

BRANDON: Thanks for your concern, but it is not any of these things you've just said. It is…

VIVIAN: It's what then?

BRANDON: I mean… [He starts to look down at the floor now.] I mean you.

VIVIAN: What about me? I hope I have done nothing wrong.

BRANDON: You did nothing wrong. It is just… I mean… I…

VIVIAN: Come on. Say what's on your mind? I might be of help to you. I know in the past that I have kept my distance, but you should know that as a woman I need to be…

BRANDON: Vivian, in fact I cherish every bit of you, and I really want you to be mine, closest of all. I really feel for you all that a man can feel for a woman in the centre of his heart. From the very first day I saw you, I've felt a change within my body, and whenever I think of you I get happy.

VIVIAN: I like you as a person to be with but we need time to become closer. We've got to learn each other's dos and don'ts and let the love build up itself, but everything has to move slowly.

BRANDON: Oh Vivian, you've brightened my world with these words. Say what you want me do to in order to let this relationship flow together by itself and bloom into the flower of love.

VIVIAN: What I want from you is to respect my person and my word and not to rush me.

BRANDON: Your word is like law set up by a government, and I will obey every part of it.

Vivian: Okay.

BRANDON: But what of Felix?

VIVIAN: Never mind. I will take care of him. In fact, we're are just friends with no strings attached, and besides he has not really told me his mind. But don't get upset by my closeness with him. I need time to explain to him about you and find a fair means to let him know he can't be around me like before.

BRANDON: All you've said is very much okay by me.

VIVIAN: I like the gentleman in you.

BRANDON: I'm really happy to hear this compliment from you. Now shall we go in and dance?

VIVIAN: Why not?

[Johnny and Susan are dancing and the party is growing. There is a lot to eat and drink. Johnny and Susan speak about the Wild Hut and both plan to meet there on Monday after work. The party swings on until late in the night, and early the next day the guests start to leave. Felix, Vivian, and Susan leave last. Brandon stays the night at Johnny's place and uses the time to tell Johnny about his discussion with Vivian and how he is looking forward to a long happy relationship with Vivian.]

CHAPTER TWO

[Brandon is being introduced to his new position in the company, and his new office is next to Felix's. At break time, Brandon goes to the café dining room, where he meets Johnny and Susan.]

BRANDON: Hi Johnny. Hello Susan.

JOHNNY: Hi Brandon, and how is your new office?

BRANDON: Oh good. I think I like it, but I miss your companionship.

JOHNNY: I do miss you too, but we can see each other every day here. Oh here comes Vivian.

BRANDON: Hi Vivian.

VIVIAN: Hi Susan. Hello Brandon, and hello Johnny.

[Vivian bends down and gives Susan a kiss on the cheek. She also gives both Johnny and Brandon a kiss.]

VIVIAN: That party was something else. I really enjoyed every bit of it: the food, the music, and in fact the whole atmosphere was just great.

BRANDON: I'm so happy you enjoyed it Vivian, and now what do you care to drink?

VIVIAN: Oh thanks, Brandon. Fruit tea, but I'd rather pay for it myself.

BRANDON: Not to worry. I bill this to myself.

SUSAN: Brandon you're a perfect gentleman. You will definitely make a good family man. It will be a lucky woman who has you in the house.

VIVIAN: Good Brandon. You've just gotten a favourable compliment from Susan. I hope you live up to it.

BRANDON: I'm just the way you see me, both in private and in public.

JOHNNY: What do you people have to say about me?

VIVIAN: Oh Johnny, you are, well, Johnny. Everything about you is just so Johnny.

BRANDON: Yes, just Johnny.

SUSAN: Yes, the one and only Johnny.

JOHNNY: What's this Johnny stuff all about?

VIVIAN: I mean that you mean a lot to me, oh to all of us in general.

BRANDON: Yes Vivian is right. You mean much to us all.

JOHNNY: Oh, time is up. I've got to go back to work. I've got a lot on my desk today.

SUSAN: I guess I should go now too.

[Susan and Johnny leave together, and Brandon and Vivian stay at lunch a little longer. As Susan and Johnny move down the hallway to their offices, Johnny asks Susan about the files on the Olympic project.]

JOHNNY: How is the Olympic project going in your department?

SUSAN: We have a lot of companies bidding for the painting, but all are the same old firms as usual with just one new applicant, a firm known as Jovans. I presume this is a new firm anyway because I never heard of it.

JOHNNY: Susan, care to go and drink with me after work.

SUSAN: Oh yes, of course.

JOHNNY: Then we'll go to the Wild Hut, but keep it a secret because you know if Vivian and Brandon hear they would want to come along, and there is something I want to discuss privately with you.

SUSAN: Okay, I will tell no one. Till then, bye.

[After work Susan and Johnny met at wild hut. At the Wild Hut.]

SUSAN: Johnny you know I like it so much here. It's really cool.

JOHNNY: For a girl as pretty as you, only a cool place like this would be appropriate to bring you in for a chat.

SUSAN: Johnny, you have a very sweet voice and are articulate. In fact, you have a very seductive manner. Men! But thanks for your compliment anyway, but you know I don't believe, or rather find it difficult to accept, the fact that you don't have a girl with all these sweet voiced and suave attributes of yours. You can sweep any girl off her feet, or are you the hit and run type, I mean the one night stand type.

JOHNNY: First what would you like to eat or drink? Waiter, please.

SUSAN: Red wine and Italian pizza please, and natural water.

Waiter: Yes please, what's your order?

JOHNNY: One glass of red wine and a glass of beer, two Italian pizzas and also two glasses of natural water.

JOHNNY: Susan, you see people seem to judge me wrongly. My words come really from my heart, so when I say you're beautiful, I mean it. And when I say I don't have any girl at the moment, I mean that as well. You see, the reason I have chosen to remain without a girl for this long is because I'm searching for the right girl that suits my life. I want a solid partner, but I think I'm close to finding that choice. But you know the big problem is I don't know if the choice will really accept me.

SUSAN: Have you really tried to tell the choice, oh I mean [*laughing*] the girl, that she is the one on your mind?

JOHNNY: No, I fear she might turn me down, and I'm the kind of guy with a fragile heart that is broken easily and I fear if its broken I might never fall in love again. That is why I am trying to speak with you about it.

SUSAN: I would like to help you, but first I don't know this choice, I mean this girl, who is on your mind. I tell you that you should walk up to her and open up to her just the way you did to me, and with your look she wouldn't say no. If she's without a boy, she can first accept you as friend, then a deeper relationship follows afterward.

JOHNNY: I'm a shy guy in speaking about my feelings to a girl I love. [*When Johnny says this word he starts to look at the table, moving is finger nervously on the surface.*]

SUSAN: Oh here comes the waitress with our order. Let's eat, then you tell me who the girl is, and if I know her then I can figure out a way to approach her on your behalf.

[Now they are eating and are both quiet for sometime, then suddenly Susan decides to break the silence.]

SUSAN: Johnny, may I ask who this girl is? Could she be someone I know?

JOHNNY: I don't know if you know her or not, but even if you do know her what will you do, and if you don't know her will you go to her on my behalf anyway if I tell you who she is?

SUSAN: Yes, I'll go to her if I do know her, tell her how you feel about her, and try to convince her to give you a chance if possible to speak to one another. In fact, I will try to fix you up with a date for the three of us, and I will speak very good of you to her. I will be able to tell, if I were in her shoes, if I would give you a chance, at least get to know you better.

JOHNNY: Oh Susan, now I know that you not only have a beautiful face and nice shape but you are very intelligent as well, and to add to all that you are kind and soft-hearted.

SUSAN: Johnny, you've been praising about my waist for some time now, but today you make me feel like a true woman of beauty with your comments Thank you Johnny for the compliment.

JOHNNY: Susan, I don't know how to thank you for taking time to sit and listen to my problem, but please, I want it to be a top secret between me and you. I want it to be a top secret. I'm shy and I fear people will laugh at me because I'm shy in woman-matters. They will say I'm brave in pushing other to go forward in approaching a woman, but me myself, I'm shy.

SUSAN: I know how you feel. I promise you I will repeat no word said here to anyone. I won't do anything to hurt your feelings. My lips are sealed about this issue discussed here. But if I may ask, who is this girl?

JOHNNY: Her name starts with an 'S.'

SUSAN: 'S'? I can't figure any name that starts with S. Please let's don't make puzzles. Tell me the name, or are you shy about saying the name?

JOHNNY: Yes, I am shy. I think I can write it on a sheet of paper and give it to you, though.

SUSAN: Okay, do that. Here is a sheet of paper and a pen to write with.

[Johnny takes the sheet from Susan and writes SUSAN on it.]

JOHNNY: Susan, here is the name.

[Susan unfolds the sheet and reads the name.]

SUSAN: SUSAN. Anyone I know?

JOHNNY: Yes.

SUSAN: Who is she?

JOHNNY: You?

SUSAN: Me? [*She looks directly into Johnny's eyes, and he shyly looks down at the table.*]

JOHNNY: I think I will go to the restroom so I can give you time to decide on what to say.

[Johnny stands up and walks to the toilet. Susan looks at him as he walks sluggishly away. Johnny looks back and sees Susan looking at him, and he looks away and then looks back again the second time, but now she is looking down on the sheet of paper Johnny gave her. Johnny goes quickly to one of the waiters and asks him to meet him by the kitchen entrance. At the entrance Johnny tells the waiter he has a music request to make, Can We Be Lovers *by Teddy Pendergrass. Johnny asks the waiter to start the music when he starts to walk back to his table and hands him five dollars.*

Johnny finishes using the toilet and as he is coming out his music request starts to be played. Now the music gets into Susan's ear and she likes the melody, and at that stage she starts to think of Johnny and of an answer to give to him. The song goes, "... so can we be lovers, can we be lovers, you're the only one for me, please be careful baby how you talk to me cause I have a fragile heart that is broken easily, and if its broken I will never love again so be careful sweet darling." Johnny catches Susan very far away and mediating on the music and on Johnny's proposal.]

JOHNNY: Hi. I'm back.

SUSAN: Oh Johnny.

JOHNNY: Surprised to see me?

SUSAN: Well, not really, only my mind is swept away by the music and your words.

JOHNNY: I'm so glad you are thinking of me, and what do you have to say?

SUSAN: Well, I can't say no to your request because you are my kind of guy, but your approach...

JOHNNY: Please say nothing more. Let's just give this

relationship a trial. You see, I don't do this very often. I spent days, weeks, and months thinking of the right way to come to you, so lets give it chance for a good free-flowing relationship to bring in an ocean of love.

SUSAN: I hope your words are your world. I don't want to come into your world and get a broken heart.

JOHNNY: My world is a world of peace and love. [He reaches out and holds Susan by the hand.] Look, I'm a lover not a fighter – one who cherishes being loved and loved back.

SUSAN: I will try to give my best and respect this relationship. Oh Vivian will be surprised to hear we are together.

JOHNNY: Sure it will be a surprise to her, but I prefer we keep this relationship a secret from everyone including Vivian and even Brandon. Do this and I'll be very happy. I've got my reason. The secrecy will just be for short time, and later we will tell them of the relationship with a big party to follow

SUSAN: I don't understand why you want to keep this relationship a secret. What is your reason?

JOHNNY: You see I'm really thinking of letting this relationship lead to a future marriage. You're the lady of my dreams, and well, about my up-coming contract to be approved by our firm for the painting of the Olympic stadium complex, you know what is involved. Financially it's not small, and any financial success is our financial success for our future. So you see, I don't want people to start talking if the contract is approved. You have been the person who holds all the applicant files involved in the painting, and people will start thinking bad things about how Jovans got awarded the contract.

SUSAN: Okay, I see your reason now, but promise we will have more time for each other.

JOHNNY: Oh, I promise we will spend every hour not used in sleeping or in working together.

SUSAN: It's late. I've got to go home now.

JOHNNY: Oh given my happiness at your accepting me, I had forgotten how late it is. Waiter, the bill please.

[Johnny pays the bill and walks Susan to her car, kisses her on the cheek, and says good-bye. Then he drives home.

At home, Johnny tells his brother about the next move and tells him never to mention to anyone about his relationship with Susan. He also tells him that the odds are now 90% that the contract for the painting of the Olympic project will be given to them.]

JOHNNY: I've got Susan, Vivian, and Brandon to stand up for Jovans' bid, so you can see our chances are very high.

CHAPTER THREE

[Johnny is very busy in his office, but in his mind is the thought of Jovans. He is thinking how happy he will be if the painting of the Olympic project is award to Jovans, and suddenly he decides to call on Brandon to ask him when the painting of the project will be approved. Johnny picks up the phone and dials Brandon's office.]

JOHNNY: Hi Brandon. It's me, Johnny.

BRANDON: Hello Johnny. I was just thinking of calling on you.

JOHNNY: How's work and your new office?

BRANDON: Well, all is moving as expected for the moment.

JOHNNY: Would you like to go with me to the Wild Hut after work?

BRANDON: Yes, of course, but I've got to tell Vivian. She said that maybe she would like to go somewhere with me.

JOHNNY: I'm happy you are together with Vivian. This is your dream come true.

BRANDON: It's all your doing Johnny, but I promise you I'll pay you back for all you've done for me.

JOHNNY: You don't have to pay me for anything back. After all, what are friends for? Oh Brandon, by the way, do you know when the company will be deliberating on what company to award the Olympic painting project to?

BRANDON: Yes, "JOVANS" I wrote on my desk calendar, "Olympic project next week: TUESDAY DECISION." But Johnny, I've got my plan for your Jovans.

JOHNNY: Really, on Tuesday. It would be better if we speak more when we meet at the Wild Hut.

BRANDON: Okay, I call Vivian, and I'll call you back later.

[Brandon calls Vivian, but she says she isn't feeling so good and that she would like to go home and sleep.]

BRANDON [*dials Johnny*]: Hello, it's me.

JOHNNY: What did Vivian say?

BRANDON: She's not feeling so good, so she would like to go home immediately after work so she can have some sleep. So I think it will be just you and me going to the Wild Hut after work.

JOHNNY: Okay. See you after work.

[Johnny later calls on Susan and fixes a date with her for 8 ' clock that evening. After work, Johnny and Brandon meet and they both drive in their own cars to the Wild Hut. At Wild Hut:]

JOHNNY: Oh I like it here. The atmosphere is something else. I'm hungry. I think I'll order fried potatoes and roasted chicken.

BRANDON: Any time I'm here I feel like eating. I think I'll order the same as you, but the entire bill is on me. Waiter, please.

WAITER: Yes, what's your order please?

JOHNNY: A big glass of orange soft drink with water, fried potatoes, and roasted chicken.

BRANDON: Apple soft drink with water.

WAITER: Big or small?

BRANDON: Medium glass, fried potatoes, and roasted chicken as well. Please waiter, do you have the music, *That's What Friends Are For*, by...by... I can't remember the actress' name.

WAITER: I think I know what you mean, and we have it. I will play it for you.

BRANDON: Thank you, and here's a tip for you.

WAITER: Thanks.

JOHNNY: Thank you Brandon. You're really a good friend, one who never forgets a good deed.

BRANDON: About the project, I'm working on a plan so that the contract can be awarded to Jovans. I have put Jovans' files first on the computer, and it will be the first to be discussed that day. I've told Vivian to stand by Jovans because she will be there in the room that day, and as usual the executive director, Mr. Barry Woods, will ask her opinion and her reasoning on all issues to be deliberated upon. Vivian is like Mr. Barry's last resort on any decision to be made.

JOHNNY: And what did Vivian say when you told her to push for Jovans?

BRANDON: She said okay, but I never told her about your connection with Jovans.

JOHNNY: Good of you, and what will your reason be for giving the contract to Jovans?

BRANDON: First, I have to point out to them what a wonderful job Jovans did on the shopping complex, and that as a new firm they will want to do the very best, make a very extraordinarily good job of it so that they can be called upon again, and then I will point out that their bid is much lower than that of the so-called big firms and that this cost reduction brings in more money for our organisation.

JOHNNY: That's good, but you must also tell Vivian to say the same thing.

BRANDON: I told her already.

JOHNNY: This is very good of you Brandon. I'm so happy to hear you standing by me and my Jovans. Oh, here comes the waiter with our food.

BRANDON: This food smells so good. I hope it tastes as delicious. Soon we will be celebrating the award of the contract to Jovans, and with this award Johnny, I think success is really coming your way. But don't you think that sooner or later our organisation will find out of your association with Jovans?

JOHNNY: If no one tells them they won't know, and all documentation is in my brother's name and signed by him, but nevertheless I think I will give a thought to quitting the organisation so that I can give more of my energy and time to Jovans. And when I resign from All Worlds, then it will mean nothing to me or to the organisation whether I'm a part of Jovans or not. But right now it's between you and me.

BRANDON: Well, it's pretty cool if it does work out that way. I know you to be a master of planning and execution. Your plans, as I well know, have never failed. I hope it works out well this time around.

JOHNNY: The main sticking point is All World awarding the contract to Jovans.

[After much discussion and eating they both drive home. At home, Johnny starts to think of the best way to convince Felix to side with Jovans, and he thinks the best person to use on Felix is Vivian. The next working day, he tells Vivian to meet him at home after work.

After work, Johnny drives home quickly to prepare and waits for Vivian, when suddenly there is a knock on the door.]

JOHNNY: Yes, who is it?

VIVIAN: Its me Vivian?

Johnny [*opens the door and lets her in*]: Oh Vivian, you look extremely beautiful in this outfit.

VIVIAN: Thanks Johnny. I'm happy you like the outfit.

JOHNNY: Not just the outfit, but your sublime person as well. [*Johnny holds her and pulls her close to him, and before she can say a word he is kissing her all over. They kiss for a long time and then fall gently on the floor of the living room and make love. Vivian says afterward that it was the first time she made love on the floor and it's the best she ever had. She tells him how much she loves him.*

Johnny tells her how much he loves her and cares about her, and about how he is planning a good future for them. He tells her to remember to stand on the side of Jovans when All Worlds decides who is to be awarded the contract of the painting of the Olympic project.]

JOHNNY: Vivian dear, if Jovans gets this contract, Jovans will grow and will be awarded future projects and we will have a prosperous future. You see, as Jovans expands, so will the family because I'll be thinking of being a father and you a mother. In fact, everything is going to expand in the right direction.

VIVIAN: Oh Johnny, you are such a darling. You've got a good plan for our a future, and on my part I'll try to do everything possible so Jovans can get the contract.

JOHNNY: But never forget, it's a secret, never let anyone know about my interest or your interest in Jovans.

VIVIAN: Johnny dear, never worry. I will take care of this and keep it top secret.

JOHNNY: Your boss, the director of the company, holds the last key to the yes or no about the issuing of the contract, and I see the way he looks at you. He seems to be interested in you, and I think he will listen to any idea you give to him. You know that when a man likes a woman anything the woman does is the right and the best thing. And the same thing also holds for Felix. Try to get him on your side.

VIVIAN: I know he likes me because he never stops telling me how nice I look when I wear that red dress, which is short, to my knees. He tells me it brings out my figure so nicely.

JOHNNY: Put on that dress more often and maybe he will ask you to go for a drink with him.

VIVIAN: I'll do anything for you Johnny. I mean for us. But with him just a drink and nothing more. You see he has asked me to go for a drink with him before, but I gave him an excuse and said no thanks.

JOHNNY: Take the opportunity if he asks again, and I'll give you the go-ahead, but don't extend your stay or go beyond the boundary of our relationship. I'm jealous, okay?

VIVIAN: I'll take care of everything. Just remember that I love you, and all I do is for you. I've already told Brandon to stand by Jovans, and I've already figured out a plan on how to handle the executive director Mr Barry. I know he will always seek my opinion on this matter, so I think I'll accept a date with him to go out for drink so I can bring up the issue. If I talk to him about it ahead of time, there will be no doubt I his mind on the day of the decision.

[Vivian comes to work the next day wearing a tight red outfit that her boss likes so much, with an expensive perfume to match. In fact, the whole room smells of her nice aroma. At nine o'clock her boss comes in. Mr Barry enters the outer office where Vivian's desk is located.]

VIVIAN: Good morning Mr Barry.

BARRY: Morning Vivian. Oh you look nice in your outfit. Is that Christine Dior I'm smelling? Oh, I love it!

VIVIAN: Yes, and thank you. Do you care for a cup of coffee?

BARRY: Nice of you to ask. I would like one. Thank you.

[Barry goes into his office and Vivian fetches the coffee.]

VIVIAN: Here is the coffee, Mr Barry.

MR BARRY: Thanks Miss Vivian. Do you care to go out to dinner with me today?

VIVIAN: Well,...em, em, em...

BARRY: Come on, just a dinner?

VIVIAN: Okay, but I must go home to change.

BARRY: No, this outfit is the best for going to dinner.

VIVIAN: Okay. If you insist.

BARRY: We will drive to the restaurant straight from work. The Hilton hotel is the place.

VIVIAN: Oh, it's expensive to eat there.

BARRY: For such an outfit, you are worth an expensive place like the Hilton hotel.

VIVIAN: Okay, after work.

[After work, Vivian and Mr Barry drive to the Hilton hotel.]

VIVIAN: I love it here. It's richly decorated.

BARRY: I love it here too. Have you checked through the menu yet? Here comes the waiter.

[They place their order, and while they are eating Mr Barry tells Vivian how beautiful she looks and how he admires her intelligence. He tells her how she has been of great assistance to him in making very difficult decisions. Vivian, hearing this, feels it's an opportunity to bring up the issue of Jovans and the Olympic project.]

VIVIAN: What do you think about giving the painting of the Olympic project to a young, new, less expensive, and hard working firm?

BARRY: Don't you think the Olympic project is too much for a new firm?

VIVIAN: This firm, Jovans, which handled the shopping complex, did marvellous work there, and on the report I read it did the work on time and for the lowest bid.

BARRY: Well, we can give them a try with a small contract perhaps.

VIVIAN: You see, we need a firm that will listen to what we say, one which we can control and will follow our work plan. I think we should give them the Olympic project.

BARRY: Okay. I think you've got a good reason, but I've got to give it some thought. I need to read more about this Jovans.

[The next day at work Vivian tells Johnny about the meeting with Mr Barry. Johnny is very happy, and he tells her how much he loves her. Tuesday of the following week is the day the company representatives meet to decide on what firm to award the contract.

On the day of the decision, everybody from Felix to Vivian, Brandon, and Susan recommended Jovans. So the contract was awarded to Jovans and the company promised to give the Parliament contract to Jovans as well if it does a very good job.

Jovans does very nice work and the Parliament project is awarded to Jovans as well. Johnny resigns from All Worlds Groups so that he can have more time for Jovans. Johnny starts thinking about how to push his brother, Evans, aside so that he can be the head of the decision-making at Jovans, or better yet how he can own the company solely himself.

Jovans is negotiating for business in far east Asia, and Johnny decides that Evans must go first and that he will join him later. While Evans was in the Far East, Evans' girlfriend's wealthy parents die in a plane crash. Johnny sees it as an opportunity to get the girl and get a part of the girl's wealth because she is an only child it is assumed she alone will inherit the estate of her dead parents. Evans, on hearing the news of the girlfriend's parent's deaths, wants to return, but Johnny asks him to stay and says that he will console her in his brother's absence. He also tells Evans that he will be coming to join him in the far east immediately after the burial, then Evans can join his girlfriend while Johnny stays behind to round up business.

At the time of the burial Irene is so down and worried because the one she thinks she loves is not around to console her, saying he is on a business trip in the Far East. Irene tells Johnny how badly she feels about Evans behaviour and thanks Johnny for caring so much and for cancelling his business trip in order to keep her company through the funeral.

Johnny criticises his brother badly and says he could never do such a thing to anyone he loves. She asks him if he thinks Evans really love her, and Johnny says he doesn't think Evans does love her and that Evans still hungers for his youthful life of changing girls regularly. Not like himself, he tells her, and that right now he is focused on having a family of his own but hasn't met someone who suit him.

At this point, Johnny makes her such a strong drink that she gets drunk immediately. Johnny tells her how he admires everything about her and always thinks about her being she his. He holds her hand and looks into her eyes, and out of confusion and drunkenness she kisses him and they make love. Later, Irene tells Johnny that she will only go into a relationship that will lead to a successful marriage. She says she doesn't know what people will say if they find out she made love with him, and as for Evans, she doesn't think she can continue with him any longer. Johnny tells her how much he wants to be with her, and he tells her they must hide their relationship from Evans and everyone else for awhile. Johnny tells her they can get married secretly and see how the marriage and the relationship will work, that marriage is like a woman owning a man all to herself and a man owning a woman to himself.

Johnny says that for him marriage is the only way he can prove his love to her. Irene, upon hearing all this, decides to give him a try, and tells him that for a long time she has admired him for his looks and the way people speak of him.

They get married secretly, and Johnny starts planning to get her pregnant so that he can hold onto her more tightly. He thinks if she gets pregnant that she will never go back to Evans or leave him. All this planning by Johnny is just to get at Irene's father's enormous wealth. Irene gets pregnant in no time.

At this time, Vivian and Susan are both pregnant by Johnny, and both Vivian and Susan are planning to keep the man responsible for their pregnancy a secret from each other. They both want to give each other a surprise.

Days later Johnny travels to the Far East to join his brother, and he tells his brother he can now go back to Europe while he takes care of some of the unfinished business and also attends an exhibition. His brother accepted the proposal and thinks it good that he can go back to his girlfriend Irene. But unknown to Evans, on the day of his departure, Johnny has already planted a huge amount of cocaine in Evans' suitcase. Johnny pretends he is sick and can not travel with his brother to the airport to see him off. Luckily for Evans he passes the Far Eastern airport unnoticed, but at Brussels airport in Belgium he is apprehended. Evans tries to argue for his innocence, but no one will believe he had nothing to do with the drugs found in his suitcase and he gets 10 years imprisonment.

Johnny never visits his brother at the Belgian prison, and he tells his wife, his brother's former girlfriend, that Evans has used drugs for a long time but Johnny didn't think he used very much. He tells her that on several occasions he told his brother to stop using drugs, and in fact he thought he had stopped, but what Johnny never knew was that Evans was dealing drugs, perhaps to support his own habit.

Irene begs Johnny not to have anything to do with Evans, because now that Johnny is handling all her father's business and has to deal with powerful people it would not be good for them or for the image of their company. Johnny pretends to feel badly about his brother's predicament, but he says he will follow his wife's advice and not have anything to do with him so that he doesn't get them involved in his drug problem. They decide to return all mail sent to them from Evans without reading it.

Evans writes lots of letters to both Johnny and Irene, but he gets no reply eventually tires of writing them, so he decides to write to Vivian and Susan. A human rights lawyer helps him with the appeal, and Vivian and Susan come to see Evans on the day of the appeal. It is found revealed at the trial that Evans' fingerprints were not on the drugs, and Evans tells them that his hotel in the Far East was shared only with his brother. Through the prosecutor's order the international police got Johnny's fingerprints, and the fingerprints were found to be the only ones on the drugs.

Johnny is indicted by the Belgian court, and he is found guilty of dealing drugs and conspiracy to implicate another person in drug charges and is then sentenced to 10 years in prison.

At Johnny's trial, Susan and Vivian find out that Johnny has been dating both of them and that they are both carrying Johnny's child. They promise to keep being best friends, but they swear never to have anything to do with Johnny. Susan and Vivian endeavour to help the young Irene, who is confused, when they discover she also carries Johnny's baby. They tell Evans to go back to Irene and take her as his wife, that the fault is not Irene's because she was brainwashed just they all were. They tell Evans that going back to Irene will definitely defeat all of Johnny's ethics devilishly wicked plans. Irene and Evans were reunited. Irene gives birth to a baby girl, and Susan and Vivian both give birth to baby boys. Johnny is serving his ten years in a Belgian prison, and Vivian starts to see Mr. Barry more often. Soon they are living happily together. Susan gets married to Brandon.

Johnny writes to Vivian while in prison and tells her that Susan got him drunk so that she could make love to him, which is how Susan got pregnant, and he tells them that his involvement in this drug issue was just a set up by his brother so that he could have their firm all by himself. Johnny also writes to Susan and tells her the same story about the drugs and that Vivian got him drunk in order to have sex with him.

Susan and Vivian get their letters from Johnny and read them together. Then they put both letters in a big envelope, along with some pictures of themselves with their husbands and a picture of Evans with Irene. They also include a short note telling him that his game is over and that they have found out what an instigator he is and none of them want anything to do with him. They tell him that they are all happy together and will all work together to figure out any of his wicked motives if he ever shows up in their lives again.

They also tell him that he will never see any of the children he has fathered.

LADYBIRD

A Play

CHAPTER ONE

[There is a poor farming family who lives in the countryside, a family of five comprised of the father, the mother, two daughters, and a son. Their dog's name is Tailor. The family makes their living by farming a small plot of land. The father's name is David, the mother is Juliet, the daughters Linda and Sandra, and the son Tim. The youngest member of the family is Sandra, and she has the likeness of a bird, with long thin legs and long aquiline nose and furtive movements as if she were always wary. She likes go to the bank of the river to watch the birds gather and perch in the trees. One Saturday evening, Tim decides to go to the bank of the river, and he asks his two sisters if they would like to go with him.]

TIM: Sandra and Linda, I would like to take a walk by the riverbank. Would anyone like to go along?

SANDRA: I think I'll go with you.

LINDA: I'd like to go too.

[And all three of them go for a walk by the bank of the river.]

SANDRA: Tim, Linda, look at all of the colourful birds that are in that tree. I love those birds. Their colours make the tree look so beautiful, and when they fly from branch to branch they make it look even more beautiful. Isn't that wonderful?

LINDA: You're right Sandra. The birds in that tree really give the tree a distinct appearance from the other trees without birds.

[Tim bends down to pick up a stone.]

TIM: I'll chase the birds away from that tree so that they can go to the other trees, so we can see how the other trees will look with birds in them.

SANDRA: No, just leave them alone. Don't you know you can hurt or even kill them? Better you just leave them alone.

TIM: Why? I don't want to kill the birds. It's just a small stone I'm throwing.

[And he throws the stone at the birds. The stone hits one and the poor bird falls to the grass.]

LINDA: Good shot, but, poor bird, I think you got her badly.

SANDRA: I hate what you just did! Tim, you don't have to stone those birds. Now you knocked one down. I will pick her up and help her.

LINDA: Sandra, why bother yourself? She will die soon.

TIM: Look Sandra, forget this bird and let's go home.

SANDRA: Just leave me alone, you bird killer!

LINDA: Sandra, just because of one bird, you're now mad at your brother.

SANDRA: You just go with Tim! Both of you, leave me alone!

[Sandra picks up the bird, wraps her up with a leaf, and takes her along home. At home, Sandra puts the bird in a carton and warms her up by placing leaves around the inside of the carton. She goes to her father to ask him what to do to save the bird from dying.]

SANDRA: Dad, Tim threw a stone at a bird and she fell, and now she is about to die. Please, can you help me? Can you tell me what to do to save the bird's life?

DAD: I'm happy you care for birds, but worrying so much about this dyeing bird is a waste of time because if she's hurt that badly she will die anyway. I think I can get you another bird if this dying bird is really disturbing you.

SANDRA: I want no other bird. I just want to save this one from dying. Can you help me with it?

DAD: Okay. Try to give her water mixed with pepper. She might be okay if she drinks it.

SANDRA: Thank you Dad. I'll go do just that. How I would love to help this poor bird live.

[Sandra goes to the bird with the preparation of water with pepper and gives it to her.

Later, Sandra prepares the bird for sleep so that she too can get some rest, but just as she is about to fall asleep a heavy thunderstorm arrives and rain begins falling. Sandra's window is blown open by the wind and she wakes up. She takes the bird to a corner of the room to prevent the wind and the cold from reaching her. As she sits on the bed and holds the bird on her lap, a huge lightning flash with a loud thunder bursts above the house, and immediately she sees only darkness. The lights in the house have gone off, and at this time the bird starts to speak to her. She is surprised and fearful, but the bird tells her not be afraid, that she, the bird, is not going to harm her. The bird thanks her for all the effort she made to save her life, but the bird says that she will be dying soon anyway. However, the birds says that she will give Sandra a special power from the bird world and that with this power she will be an extraordinarily strong young woman, one who will do impossible things, one who will save animals and mankind from a danger that will arrive soon.

The bird tells Sandra that she's not just an ordinary bird, that she is the princess of the birds and her name is Ladybird. Whenever Sandra wants that special power, the bird tells her that she just has to say "from Ladybird with love," but she is never to use this power for evil or to harm anyone, or for any other bad thing whatsoever.

There are repercussions when the power is used negatively, and that repercussion is death. And the bird tells Sandra one more thing: when she is on the bank of the river or in water she must never let a stone touch your armpit because if this happens her power will be lost and she might die. But if a prince kisses her on the lips after the stone has touched her armpit, then Sandra would not die from it. She now pronounces Sandra Ladybird, the princess of all birds, and then the bird dies with those last words.]

SANDRA: Oh Ladybird, don't die now please. Stay with me a little. [Sandra is now full of tears, but the bird is already dead.

Sandra takes the bird outside the next day and buries her. The following day, Sandra goes to school and is filled with thoughts of the bird and what the bird told her. [*Sandra's best friend in school, Joyce, catches Sandra far away in thought.*]

Joyce: Hi Sandra. I could see you are far away.

SANDRA: Oh Joyce, you're right. I'm far away in thought.

Joyce: And what has carried you so far away?

SANDRA: Not so serious a matter really. Never mind.

[Joyce and Sandra go to Joyce's home, which is a two-story building. As they approach the house they hear a child crying loudly.]

SANDRA: Joyce I can hear a child crying. I think it's your brother Kelvin. [*Kelvin is just two years old.*]

Joyce: It sounds just like him, but what on earth could be making him cry out so loudly.

SANDRA: Look Joyce! What am I seeing by the balcony up on the last floor?

Joyce: That's Kelvin and I think he's stuck between the poles, but how on earth did he get up there alone? Oh, he seems to be falling with his head facing downward. Come on, let's rush to help him. [As they get to the boy, Sandra tells Joyce to go inside and alert her parents so that they can try to get him down from up there. She says that she will wait for her and keep the child still by talking to him, because if he moves very much he could slip and fall. As Joyce went inside, Sandra quickly says the Ladybird words: "from Ladybird with love." As she says this she immediately starts to rise up until she gets to where the little boy. She removes him from between the poles and carries him down to safety. As she lands with Kelvin, Joyce and her parents arrive at the balcony and they can not find Kelvin. When they look down, they see Kelvin playing happily with Sandra. Her parents just look at Joyce and shake their heads. As her parents leave the balcony, they tell Joyce never to use such serious matters as a joke again, but she insists she was not joking, that Kelvin was really up there. They just leave Joyce and go into the living room. Joyce now goes out to meet Sandra and Kelvin to ask what happened.]

Joyce: Sandra, did Kelvin fall? Is he hurt?

SANDRA: No. I mean, yes he did fall and I caught him in my hands.

Joyce: Isn't he hurt from such a fall, and you, your hands should hurt you badly. I should call Papa and Mama so we can take you both to the hospital.

SANDRA: I'm okay, just a little pain. It doesn't really hurt that badly, and I think he is okay because I caught him perfectly well. Just watch how he is jumping. He has already forgotten what happened, but taking him to the hospital is not a bad idea, just for a medical check because of the height he fell from and his age.

Joyce: But my parents don't seem to believe Kelvin was up there, and now he is right down here unharmed. They think I just wanted to play a joke on them.

SANDRA: I know it's hard to believe how he fell unhurt, but what matters most is that he is down here playing now unhurt.

[Sandra leaves Joyce and goes home. It is 5 o'clock in the evening when she gets home. She eats her food and then she takes some of the bird food she bought previously and goes to the bank of the river to feed the birds.

The next day Sandra goes to school, and as she approaches the school she sees a man falling down from the top of the highest building on the school grounds. As she watches the man falling, four faces look down over the edge of the building to watch the falling man, but as she looks at them, they raise up there hands in a form of celebration and immediately the four men disappear. Sandra knew this was apparently an attack on the falling man. Sandra quickly says the Ladybird words, 'from Ladybird with love,' and she immediately starts rising up. She flies in the direction of the falling man, catches him, and brings him to the ground safely. As they touch down, she quickly takes him away from that vacinity because she knows his attackers will come looking for him. Once she has the man safely away from that vacinity, the young man of Asian origin starts to thank her. Sandra tells him never to mention to anyone how she helped him and he promises he won't. He tells her he was attacked by a group of white boys who told him he must get out of here and go back to Asia. Sandra tells him to take care and to watch where he goes. He quickly introduces himself to Sandra as Rakim and asks Sandra her name. Then they start to walk away together.]

Rakim: Em…. Please, can I see you again?

SANDRA: For what?
Rakim: To go out for a drink.
SANDRA: No thanks.
Rakim: But…
SANDRA: Just forget about me.

Sandra walks into the school and the Asian boy follows her. As they get into the school, the four white boys who pushed Rakim from the top of the building are standing at the gate, and when they see him coming they start to ask one another if this can be the same boy they pushed from the roof. One says that he thinks the pushed boy died because they heard no cry and no ambulance siren rushing to the site, and another of the boys says this Asian boy is walking normally, not like one who fell from such a high building. Perhaps he has a twin brother who looks exactly like him, suggest another. One says that he thinks this Asian boy has the black power magic usually possessed by the Asians and the Africans. Another says that his father told him about their so-call black power, and that is why they must not be accepted here in this country. One of the boys says that it could be the Asian boy's ghost, which has probably come back to take revenge on them. Rakim walks pass them and just says hi, but they are too afraid to reply. They just back away with fear written on the faces.

Rakim goes to lecture after lecture, then he goes home, and all the while the thought of Sandra is on his mind. He thinks how beautiful she looks and also how she possesses such an extraordinary power. And on top of everything, she is kind and good-hearted. Then he remembers that thinking of a girl from a country other than his own is forbidden for a prince like himself, because the tradition of his homeland says that he must marry a princess or someone with a royal background and that she must come from his own part of the world. But this girl of wonder, Sandra, continues to disturb his mind.

The next day being the weekend, he plans to take a walk on the hillside to have some fresh air. On the weekend, the hill is usually packed with families and students.

When Sandra gets home after school, she eats and goes straight to bed, but she can not sleep because of her fear that the Asian man, Rakim, might go about telling people about her extraordinary attribute. She thinks of three ways out: one is threaten him, two is leaving the school, and three is making friends with him. She thinks to threaten him is cruel and bad, and leaving school is really silly because she might find it difficult to get into another school, so she thinks to befriend him is best — "but men, she thinks, he will see this as an opportunity for quick sex. No way. I think I'll just leave him alone, because even if he does tell people, who on earth will believe such a fantasy story?]

Sandra sleeps off and on, and when she wakes up the next day she decides to go up the hillside at noon to take a walk and have some fresh air. Sandra picks up the phone and calls Joyce.]

SANDRA: Hello.

JOYCE'S MOTHER: Hello. Who's on the line?

SANDRA: It's me, Sandra. Please, is Joyce around?

Joyce's mother: Yes, she is right beside me.

SANDRA: Please, can I speak with her?

JOYCE'S MOTHER: I'll give her the phone. Joyce, Sandra on the line for you.

JOYCE: Hello Sandra.

SANDRA: Hello Joyce. You care to take a walk with me up the hill?

JOYCE: I'd love to. I'll come over to your place, then we can go together.

SANDRA: Good. That will be nice. I'll be expecting you then.

Joyce arrives at Sandra's place in 30 minutes, and together they go up to the hill. At the hill there is a big restaurant, and they both decide to sit there and have a drink.

SANDRA: Joyce, I love the atmosphere here. It's so natural and the air is so fresh.

JOYCE: City life is just something else, what with the smoke from the cars and the noise, but here you feel you're on holiday at a royal castle built on a hill in a reserve.

[As they are drinking, they hear noises.]

SANDRA: Joyce, I think I can hear people screaming.

JOYCE: Yes, I can hear it too, and I think it's coming from the other side of the hill where the people usually park their cars.

SANDRA: Maybe one of these families who drove a car here has left a child inside the car and the car is now rolling down the hill. Oh I must use the toilet. I'm badly stressed.

JOYCE: Sandra, when you finish, meet me outside. I'll rush out and see what is going on.

SANDRA: Okay. I will be with you in a moment.

[Joyce goes outside, and Sandra goes inside the toilet where she immediately says the Ladybird words. She moves in an electrified fast-speed manner, for with her extraordinary power she knows where the incident is and she takes the exit on the opposite side of the building from the exit Joyce used. In no time she is in front of the car, makes her way to the door of the car, gets the car door open. Then she gets behind the wheel and steers the car to the corner of the hill and parks the car safely, puts hand brake on, and quickly runs back

to the restaurant. Now she starts walking back in the direction of the crowd where the incident happened. The people there are all standing in astonishment, wondering what happened, as Joyce sees her coming, she quickly runs toward Sandra.]

JOYCE: Sandra, you won't believe it! That car was rolling very fast down the hill, and all of a sudden the door of the car was open and the car swung to the left. All of us watching thought the car fell off the hill, but to everybody's surprise this car rolled to a stop at the edge of the parking lot facing that rock. If that car fell or rolled down it would be totally disastrous for the baby inside and also for the people on the ground below, but miraculously the car stopped. Look Sandra, I know if you don't see this yourself it is very difficult to believe what happened.

SANDRA: Oh I would have loved to see this myself, this unbelievable deed with my own eyes.

JOYCE: Look, that Asian man standing over there and the parents of the child saw it too. Can we go towards them so you can hear them speaking about it?

[Sandra sees the Asian man, and she knows that if he sees her, he will know it was her who saved the car; but before she can refuse Joyce's request, the Asian boy sees her and waves and says hello.]

JOYCE: Sandra, do you know him?

SANDRA: Yes, I met him the last time I was at the school.

RAKIM: Hello Sandra.

SANDRA: Hello. [*She looks at him with a warning in her eyes.*]

RAKIM: I have to go. I'm going jogging.

JOYCE: Oh, such a good-looking guy, Sandra. I hope

he is not yours because I can see the way you both looked at each other… or….

SANDRA: He is not what you think, and we did nothing but talk for a minute. I only saw him last week at school.

JOYCE: I can see he likes you from the way he looks into your eyes, but he definitely looks good.

SANDRA: Do you like him?

JOYCE: Oh, I don't know him.

SANDRA: Come on, let's go inside the restaurant. They are playing nice music.

[They go back to the restaurant and thereafter go home. At home, Sandra starts thinking of a way to handle this Rakim issue, and now Joyce knows him and she seems to admire his looks, which complicates things.

The next day at school Sandra is taking a walk round the school and suddenly she hears someone say hi from behind. She turns around and it is Rakim.]

SANDRA: Hi.

RAKIM: You look nice in this outfit.

SANDRA: Thanks.

RAKIM: You care if we go for a drink together?

SANDRA: Em… Em…

RAKIM: Please, just a drink, nothing more.

SANDRA: Okay.

[They go to a restaurant nearby.]

RAKIM: Oh the life here is quite different from what I have in my hometown, but I like it here.

SANDRA: But how are you coping with the system here?

RAKIM: I'm getting used to every system, only for something I don't like here is the racial problem, like how I was attacked by those…

SANDRA: I know what happened to you last time.

RAKIM: But if not for you I would have…

SANDRA: It's okay. Like I told you, I want that story to be between the two of us.

RAKIM: Okay. I won't say anything about it to anyone, but how come you possess such...

SANDRA: Look, I don't want to speak about it.

RAKIM: But your friend knows, because of the incident at park hill with the little child in the rolling car.

SANDRA: She doesn't know anything about my involvement.

RAKIM: But you saved the child in that car and she was there.

SANDRA: Look, I said she did not see me do it. I think that I better go. I hate this discussion with you.

RAKIM: I'm sorry. I won't say a word of it again.

SANDRA: Okay, but say nothing of any of this to my friend Joyce especially.

Rakim: I will say nothing to her. I don't even know her. That day at the park was the first time I met her, but she has a nice name, Joyce.

SANDRA: Oh? Do you like her?

RAKIM: Not at all. Oh, here she comes now.

SANDRA: Hello Joyce.

JOYCE: Hi Sandra, and hi...

SANDRA: Oh Joyce, meet Rakim. Rakim, this is Joyce, my very good friend.

RAKIM: Pleased to meet you.

JOYCE: Rakim, where are you from?

RAKIM: Suva Island in Asia.

JOYCE: I never heard of this island.

RAKIM: It's a small island. Oh, I think I should go now. Bye girls.

SANDRA: Rakim, I'll check on you tomorrow.

RAKIM: That will be nice of you. Bye [*and he leaves.*]

JOYCE: You and he seem to be getting along well.

SANDRA: We are friends, just friends.

JOYCE: Just friends, and such a nice looking guy.

SANDRA: Hey girl, he is just a friend.

JOYCE: Soon I will start seeing the good of you two as friends, but to be honest, you're a perfect match.

SANDRA: Let's forget this issue. What are you doing after school tomorrow?

JOYCE: Clever. You see how you waved away the issue of the two of you. Anyway, after school I'm doing nothing.

SANDRA: Would you like to go jogging with me?

JOYCE: Why not? I'd love to.

SANDRA: Okay. I'll catch up with you later, at 4 o'clock.

CHAPTER TWO

[Sandra is at Joyce's place at 4 o'clock the next day. As they are jogging along, they chat much, but Joyce seems to be speaking a lot about this Rakim guy.]

JOYCE: Sandra don't you think this Rakim is so handsome and gentle.

SANDRA: Handsome, maybe. But how do you know he is gentle?

JOYCE: You can see it in his face and the manner in which he speaks.

SANDRA: But you've just met him and you are already crazy about him.

JOYCE: Oh don't get me wrong. I know he is the guy for you, or don't you want him. As for me, I don't mind, in case you aren't interested I'm ever ready to…

SANDRA: What are you ready for? Well, let's just forget about this Rakim issue. I think I'm hungry. Shall we go to the snack shop to buy something to eat?

JOYCE: Why not?

[They both go to the snack shop, eat, and later go home. In the days that follow, Rakim is seen more often in the company of Sandra and Joyce, and other students always look in astonishment and wonder what two beautiful girls are doing with this poor Asian student. They sometimes insult or make fun of Rakim, but Sandra and Joyce

always come to his rescue. One day, while with Rakim, Sandra and Joyce are at the cafeteria, and Joyce decides to ask Rakim what he does to keep himself going in the school financially.]

SANDRA: Joyce, you know it's expensive if one should develop the habit of always coming here to eat often.

JOYCE: Sandra, you complain a lot, but this whole week Rakim has been paying for our drinks.

SANDRA: Don't you think that's quite an expense for him.

JOYCE: I never hear him complaining, but Rakim what did you do to get the money that you just spent on our drinks all week?

RAKIM: I do some cleaning work after school.

SANDRA: That's a hard program, combining studies and work.

RAKIM: But I have to do it to keep going.

SANDRA: Then you don't have to throw away the money on drinks for us. You need your money for your upkeep. Look, Joyce and I have our parents here to take care of our financial needs, but you do your finances yourself, so you need to save your money.

JOYCE: Rakim, Sandra is right. You've got to save your money for yourself.

RAKIM: I know I need the money, but it makes me feel happier if I am able to take you out, Sandra, I mean take you two out for a drink.

SANDRA: I'd feel much better if you saved your money for your unforeseen expenses.

RAKIM: I've planned that out already. Look girls, you see that guy over there, the one with the white shirt. He's got a blue face cap on. I think he's coming towards our table.

SANDRA: What's with him?

RAKIM: He always calls me stupid names, telling me

that European girls and European schools are for Europeans.

JOYCE: Oh, he's called John and he is a big racist. He belongs to a racial gang. His sister is in my class, and she is so nice and liberal minded, completely the opposite of him. He's a bully, and he once asked me out, but I cant go out with such a....

SANDRA: But why is he coming towards us? I hope he doesn't make a scene here.

RAKIM: Come on girls, let's go. Or at least I better leave you two here and go. I think it's because of me that he's coming, and I don't want problems.

JOYCE: Go nowhere Rakim. Sandra and I will tell him off.

JOHN: Hey you, Asian boy, I thought I told you that this ground you're stepping on belongs to the Indigenous. Why are you trying to make things difficult for yourself here? You came to my land, came to my school, drank my drinks, and now you come on to my sisters.

JOYCE: Look John, I'm not your sister and I think Sandra is not yours as well. Just go away and leave Rakim alone, and stop being a baby racist.

SANDRA: Look John, why don't you stop this awkward behaviour of yours?

JOYCE: Oh, here comes your sister. I'll call her over to speak sense to you. Hello. Hello, Vivian. Excuse me for a moment.

VIVIAN: Hello Joyce. I hope there is no problem.

JOYCE: It's your brother John. I don't know why he thinks Rakim shouldn't be sitting with us here.

VIVIAN: John, see how you are fooling yourself? You are only being jealous of the boy with two girls. Look, you can systematically and intelligently sit happily with them and chat up one of the girls, or you better go elsewhere and look for a girl. Or do you like Rakim? I don't think he is gay, but I don't have a problem if you are gay and are merely looking for a boyfriend or lover. Just stop spoiling other people's happiness.

[John just hisses at his sister and walks away sluggishly.]

SANDRA: Thanks…em...

VIVIAN: Call me Vivian.

SANDRA: Thanks Vivian.

VIVIAN: Don't mention it. He is my younger brother and needs me to put him in line sometimes.

JOYCE: Vivian, see you later in class.

[After this incident, Rakim becomes more and more close to Sandra, and both are increasingly happy when they are together. They meet frequently after school, always by the bank of the river. One day, while they are at the river, they hear a dog barking, and when they stand up to look they see a dog being carried away by the moving water. Immediately Rakim and Sandra rush to help the poor dog. Rakim can't swim, but Sandra can so she dives into the water to rescue the dog. Rakim watches as she gets hold of the dog and drags the animal to the edge of the river. Rakim stretches out his hand and takes the dog from her so that she can climb out of the water herself. As Rakim takes the dog a safe distance from the water and puts the dog down in the grass, Sandra calls out to him to give her a helping hand out of the water. As Rakim runs to her, he steps on a flat piece of driftwood on the ground and the wood throws a quantity of small stones into the air. He sees one of the flying stones hit Sandra directly in the armpit as she has already raised her hand fully to hold onto a branch from a small tree. As the stone hits her in the armpit, she immediately falls back into the water.

Rakim quickly rushes to her and climbs into

the water, which is not so deep here that he can not stand up easily. Rakim quickly pulls Sandra out of the water. He lays her flat on her back, and she isn't moving. She just lays motionless and breathless like she is dead. Rakim becomes afraid, and the only treatment he can remember from his first-aid lessons is mouth-to-mouth resuscitation. He remembers mouth-to-mouth because at school they laughed over the procedure and called it a chance to have a good kiss.

But right now he is confused. What if he does this to her and it doesn't help, or if it helps she might be mad at him for putting his mouth to hers, and after this she might not want to see him again. But he realises that the most important thing right now is saving her life. So he bends down put his mouth onto her mouth, holds her nose, and pushes in the first breath. After only a single breath, Sandra wakes up and holds him in her arms. To his surprise, she tells him that he certainly must be a prince. He is shocked to hear this because he has never told her, or anyone else for that matter, about his royal rank.]

SANDRA: Oh my head hurts me. Rakim, why didn't you tell me that you are royalty?

RAKIM: But how do you know I'm a prince now, and are you sure you are completely okay? I just tried mouth-to-mouth resuscitation on you because for awhile you just lay there, motionless, and all I could remember is do was mouth-to-mouth.

SANDRA: You lied to me.

RAKIM: No, I'm not lying to you. It was not my intention to kiss you.

SANDRA: That's not what I mean. I'm talking about you not telling me about yourself, that you're a prince.

RAKIM: I'm sorry. I just don't want people to start

treating me differently. That's why I hid it, but how do you know?

[Sandra now tells him the Ladybird story, how she got the power and how she must be saved in the event a stone hits her on the armpit when she is by the water or in the water. After the events of this day, they fall in love with each other. Rakim now calls his father the king and tells him that he is coming back home to get married, but he does not tell his father that the girl he wants to marry is a European he met at his school. After school one day, Rakim decides to ask Sandra the big question.]

RAKIM: Sandra, baby….

SANDRA: Yes, what is it you would like to say.

RAKIM: How do you know I want to say something?

SANDRA: Because whenever you call me Sandra baby and just stop, I know that something has to follow but its something hard to say or you've not found the right words to use yet.

RAKIM: You see, each and every day I love you more and more. You've got everything a man like me wants in a woman, and on top of your other excellent qualities, you've got a good sense of humour.

SANDRA: Thanks honey, but what is it that you really want to say?

RAKIM: Okay, you win dear. I don't think I can find the right words to say this subtly, so now I will say it in a crude form: em….em …em.

SANDRA: Stop this stuttering and just say it. Don't keep me in suspense.

RAKIM: Please, would you ma…. ma …..ma …marry me?

SANDRA: Honey, yes, with all my heart. I will marry you, but…

RAKIM: But what?

SANDRA: You're a prince, and I always thought that a prince must marry a princess.

RAKIM: Sandra, you are my princess.

Sandra—But I'm an European and your father the King might not agree to your marry me

RAKIM: What matters to me now is not what my father thinks or if he agrees with my choice, but my love for you and us being together as husband and wife.

SANDRA: How will you make him understand?

RAKIM: Well, he just has to understand. You're part of this global race, the human race, and not an object fallen from outer space.

SANDRA: My mind tells me your father is going to make a hell of a lot of problems for us.

RAKIM: My mind tells me I'm going to live my life with you and not my father, and do you know the thing my mind says most?

SANDRA: No dear, what?

RAKIM: My mind is telling me that no matter what my father thinks or says I just can't stop loving you.

[Now they are approaching the wood that leads to riverbank.]

SANDRA: Rakim, what if your father says you must give up your princeship if you insist on marrying me? And you know your tradition doesn't allow girls to become King, and you've got just sister no brother. Think of it Rakim, you are the only son. Don't you think your family will lose the right to the kingship if you marry me?

RAKIM: Look Sandra, I love you so much I would give up anything, both kingship and princeship.

SANDRA: You will do all this for my sake?

[Now they are out of sight of all eyes. They are in the woods.]

SANDRA: Rakim, close your eyes. I would like to show

you something. You've seen it before, but now I want you to see and feel it in the name of love and not of fear as when you saw it before.

[Sandra pulls him close to her, his hand in her hand, and she whispers in his ear, "from Ladybird with love." As she finishes saying this, they both rise up and up and up until they are higher than the trees and all the surrounding area can be seen below their feet. Sandra asks him to open his eyes. He opens his eyes and is astonished by what he sees. After some time, Sandra asks him to close his eyes again, and when he closes his eyes they descend until their feet touch the ground again. Then she asks him to open his eye.]

RAKIM: Oh that was wonderful.

SANDRA: But it's not your first time. The last time, when I rescued you from falling, didn't you feel the same way?

RAKIM: Not the same way. That experience included fear. This one had a natural feeling of happiness and of nature itself.

SANDRA: Yes, that's the difference, fear and happiness, and that's why you closed your eyes so that the power of nature could be felt within you and fear is push away. You see nothing to bring you fear.

RAKIM: Sandra, you are my everything and my everything is you, not because of what you can do but because of what my love is burning with.

SANDRA: What is your love burning with?

RAKIM: My love is burning with desire for you. Sandra, I love you from the very bottom of my heart. I love with all the human particles a heart is made off.

SANDRA: Really?

RAKIM: Come close to my heart. Put your ear on my chest and you will hear the burning deep inside me.

[Sandra puts her ear on Rakim's chest, but before she can say a word he starts to kiss her all over.]

SANDRA [*jokingly*]: I thought in the beginning it was Joyce you wanted.

RAKIM: In the beginning, it was you and it will always be you until death do us part. Okay, I'll call my father tomorrow and fix a date for us to see my father to speak with him about our marriage.

SANDRA: I will tell my family as well.

RAKIM: But how come your parents are not bothered about you marrying someone from a different race?

SANDRA: What matters to them is my happiness, and I'm happy with you and they know that.

RAKIM: I hope my parents will think like your parents. Our happiness should come first, before princeship, but they must either understand this or they stop knowing me.

SANDRA: I don't want our marriage to hurt your relationship with your father.

RAKIM: You're not marrying me can break my relationship with my father because I already love you with all my all.

SANDRA: Rakim, I can't do without you.

RAKIM: We are meant for each other, just like my father is meant for my mother, so I'll call my father and fix a date for our visit.

CHAPTER THREE

[They meet at the park the next day. Rakim tells Sandra he has called his father and that they will meet with him in three days. He says that tomorrow they will be doing some shopping to buy clothes and other things they will need. Sandra asks Rakim if she needs to buy Asian clothes to suit his parents, but Rakim asks her to buy and wear whatever she feels is best for her. He tells her he wants her parents to accept her for the way she is and not for the way the parents want her to look. The next day they go shopping. They buy a lot of things, but Sandra complains that Rakim is spending too much on her clothing. He insists on spending the money, however. He tells her that his father sent him the money to spend and not to bring back home.]

SANDRA: Rakim, what you've bought for me is very nice. Shall we now book our tickets with the travel agency?

RAKIM: We don't need tickets. Oh, here comes your friend Joyce.

JOYCE: Hi Sandra. Hello Rakim.

SANDRA: Hello Joyce.

RAKIM: Hi Joyce.

JOYCE: When are you two travelling to Rakim's place? I wish I could come along.

RAKIM: Do you really want to come along? I think it would be nice if you come so you can keep Sandra company if I'm preoccupied ironing out issues with my father.

SANDRA: Joyce, I'm really glad you'd like to come along.

RAKIM: Okay Joyce, as you are coming along, here is some money to do some shopping.

JOYCE: So much money! I never thought I'd hold such a huge amount of money in my hand.

RAKIM: Joyce, in life you can touch whatever you wish. Why don't you start your shopping now?

SANDRA: We will now book tickets for three people.

RAKIM: We are not going to book any tickets. The royal jet is coming to pick us up.

JOYCE: Oh my God, me in a royal jet. It's all happening like magic, or maybe I'm I dreaming.

SANDRA: It's unbelievable for me because the first day I saw him I never would have guessed him to be a royal boy.

RAKIM: I decided to keep my royalty a secret so that people will accept me for who I am and not what I am.

JOYCE: If I take this whole shopping spree home, my parents will think I robbed a bank, but I will tell them it's from Prince Rakim.

SANDRA: Joyce, I don't want people to start running towards us or start flashing cameras at us.

RAKIM: It's better we leave very early tomorrow morning before people and the press can start approaching us. They will know something is up when news of the royal jet's arrival gets around.

SANDRA: That is a good idea, so Joyce, you put up with us in our hotel.

JOYCE: But I must rush home first to tell them I'm travelling to Asia with you two.

SANDRA: Okay.

[Sandra and Rakim go to their hotel and Joyce joins them later. They travel to Asia the following morning and are given a royal welcome upon their

arrival at the airport. Everybody at the airport is in a joyous mood because Rakim's homecoming will be followed by his marriage.

Sandra and Joyce are staying in the King's guesthouse. It is situated in the same area as the royal palace. Rakim stay all day long at the royal guest lodge with them and later leaves them to discuss things with his father.]

RAKIM: Sandra, I've got to see my father so that he and I can iron out certain issues.

SANDRA: About me? I mean us?

RAKIM: Yes, and other things as well.

JOYCE: Oh its really going to be tough to iron this out because I saw the look on your father's face when he saw us coming.

RAKIM: Don't let that bother you. My father always looks at someone he doesn't know in a special way, but I don't think that either of you are a problem for him.

SANDRA: I hope not, because I don't want to be a problem for your family and for your people.

JOYCE: Sandra, Rakim says that all is okay, so lets accept that.

RAKIM: Look Sandra, I love you and I won't let anything come between us, not even my father. It's you I want and you I love. [Rakim goes over to Sandra, holds her, and kisses her deeply. Then he whispers into her ear:] I love you a million times over.

[Rakim goes to the palace and is greeted by his father and mother. They ask him how he has been doing in Europe and if he's not tired from the long flight to the Far East Asia. He says he isn't tired, and his father asks him why he is not wearing his royal dress. His father tells him that as a prince of the kingdom he must not put on such clothes as he is now wearing a pair of tight jeans and a

sleeve-less shirt and a baseball cap. His mother tells his father to leave him alone about his clothes, tells him that if he is happy with his clothes then let him wear them. His father tells him that he is to be married in a week's time and that they have plans with the bride's parents, and the woman Rakim is to marry will be coming to introduce herself to him tomorrow. His father informs him that she is from a far away island and she is very beautiful.]

RAKIM: Papa, I don't need anybody to find me a wife. I've got someone with me whom I want to marry, and I love her and she loves me too.

KING: Look son, what do you know about love? Besides, tradition doesn't permit you to marry any girl you meet or a girl from anywhere.

RAKIM: Papa. She is not just any girl. I know her from school and we are always together. We love each other.

KING: Look son, you are out of your mind. Do you know what you are talking about? How come you want treat your royal lineage so lowly? We send you for a Western education, and maybe you could find a girl who can help you with your administrative work when you ascend the thrown, but now you want to marry?

RAKIM: And what is wrong with my marrying her, Papa? Mama?

MOTHER [Queen]: Son, we want only the best for you.

RAKIM: Mother, I've found the person who is best for me.

KING: Nonsense! Somebody subordinate under you, who should be serving you? And to think we spent the royal money to educate you overseas. I'll send that girl and her family off of this island and into a life exile.

RAKIM: Papa, do nothing of the kind! Just leave that girl and her family alone!

[Quickly, the king calls his bodyguard.]

ROYAL GUARD: Your Highness.

KING: Get Limbo, the chief priest. He has betrayed me.

RAKIM: No, leave them alone. They did nothing wrong.

KING: I said bring them, you fool.

RAKIM: Papa, this is not the girl I want to marry. My love is one of the girls who came with me from Europe.

KING: Look …never... you must be joking!

[Rakim leaves the palace. His father calls him back, but he says he is going to take a walk by the waterside to do some thinking. His father shouts at him to come back, but his mother tells his father to let him go, that maybe he is going to do some good thinking and perhaps change his mind about who he should marry.]

KING: He better think long and hard about this decision, and change his mind fast!

[As Rakim leaves the palace grounds, the king leaves to visit the royal guesthouse. As he arrives in the royal guesthouse, Sandra and Joyce greet him, but he just waves at them impatiently with his bodyguard standing by his side.]

KING: Which of you is having an affair with my son, Prince Rakim?

JOYCE: But King…. Well I don't know what to say to you. We just greeted you and you didn't answer us. You just waved off our greeting.

BODYGUARD: When greeting the king you must bow low. It's a tradition here. No one stays seated and greets the king in a relaxed and familiar fashion like you just did.

JOYCE: Well our tradition in Europe doesn't require us to bow down for anyone.

BODYGUARD: Rubbish. Shut up. You don't say such things in front of the king. He can order your arrest.

JOYCE: Look, I have my right to speak.

SANDRA: Okay, enough of this. Back to the king's question about who Rakim happens to be involved with.

BODYGUARD: Say Prince Rakim and not merely Rakim.

KING: That's okay. Let her finish.

SANDRA: Rakim and I feel deeply for each other.

KING: Rubbish! Forget any feelings you have for my son. He doesn't have to associate himself with people like you.

JOYCE: What are you saying this for?

SANDRA: Please Joyce, let him finish.

KING: Thank you. You seem to be a cool-headed young woman, but my son is above your station and his royal heritage doesn't permit him to mingle with your type.

[Sandra is now crying.]

JOYCE: Hey, don't say that to her. You're making her cry. [*Joyce moves toward the king, and the bodyguard stops her and holds her tightly by the arm.*]

KING: Look, I'll pay you two to leave my son alone and go back to Europe right away.

JOYCE: We don't need your money, and we are going back right away anyway.

KING: Right. I'll give you two thousand US dollar and a cheque for one million dollars as well, and here is a first class ticket for your return. It has already been confirmed for today. The flight leaves in three hours time. The palace guard will take you to the airport.

JOYCE: Sandra, stop crying, and look King, we don't need your money or your ticket or your guards to take us to the airport. We are going on our own and we are leaving right now.

SANDRA: Yes, we will leave right away.

[The king signals the bodyguard to drop the money, the cheque, and the ticket for them on the table and the king leaves.]

It's now 3.30 in the afternoon and the king always goes skydiving at this time of day. Now Joyce and Sandra have both packed and are leaving the palace guesthouse. They take a cab to a hotel far away from the royal area. The hotel is on the west side of the island and very close to the airstrip where the small planes land and take off. The hotel the cab driver takes them to is where Western tourists stay, and it's the tallest building in the country.

Joyce and Sandra get a room on the top-most floor and have already bought tickets to take them out of the country tomorrow. Now in the hotel room, Joyce decides to take a bath and Sandra goes out on the balcony to have a total view of the city. Once outside, her thoughts are only of Rakim and why Rakim has not come looking for her. Why didn't he come back to the royal palace? His father said he must not mingle with people like me, so perhaps Rakim is standing in agreement with his father. But she remembers his vows of love and of choosing love over tradition, and certainly he would have come to tell her if had changed his mind himself. Screaming stirs her from her thoughts and she immediately comes back to reality. She looks around to see where the screaming is coming from, and she figures out that it is coming from up the sky. Someone is falling down from the sky and a plane is roving over spot on the balcony. She notices the falling fellow is having problems with his parachute. Sandra quickly says the Ladybird words, 'from Ladybird with love,' and immediately she is in the sky. She holds on to the falling man, and she is surprised to discover it is the king. She takes him down to safety and quickly goes away. He starts shouting for her to come back, that she has saved his life, but she just walks away quickly.

The king is now surrounded by his bodyguards, and the king tells them a woman brought him down to safety. His adviser says that it could have been one of the angels that keep guard over kings, but the king says that he knows it was not an angel. It's someone I have met before. I know the face, but I'm not too sure of her identity. Drive me back to the palace. I've got to see my son and the queen. His adviser asks him: if he finds this girl, will he marry her? The king says he doesn't know, but the adviser tells the king he shouldn't think of marrying right now because the prince's marriage is already been planned and tradition doesn't allow both the king and prince to marry in the same year.]

KING: Look, my trusted adviser, leave the decision to me.

ADVISER: But this lady-hero could be a foreigner, and the tradition…

KING: Please leave me alone with my thoughts. I want to do some thinking.

ADVISER: Okay your highness.

CHAPTER FOUR

[The entourage arrives at the royal palace and the king quickly asks them to look for Prince Rakim]

KING: Queen dear, something ridiculous happened today. I could have died today. I was falling headfirst while doing my sky diving.

QUEEN: But you had your parachute on.

KING: Yes, I had the parachute, but I pulled the cord incorrectly and the pin got bent and refused to shoot out. I just continued to fall head first toward the ground until a lady rescued me, plucked me right out of the sky and brought me down, and the most interesting thing is that she had no parachute on.

QUEEN: Miraculous, and who is this lady.

KING: I'm not too sure, but she looked like one of the ladies who came with Rakim from Europe, but I don't think it was the one Rakim says he wants to marry.

QUEEN: How do you know its not the one Rakim wants to marry?

KING: I told them to leave for Europe earlier, that my son can not associate with them, and during my speaking with them the one Rakim wants to marry spoke and acted quietly but the other one spoke and acted without fears. So I think that only the one without fear could possess this kind of European magic.

QUEEN: I think you're right. It must be the fearless one, and what do you plan to do for her for saving your life?

KING: I don't know because I gave them a ticket to go back to Europe and the flight left ten minute ago.

QUEEN: Then it could not have been one of them, and besides the airport is in the opposite direction to the city, and almost nearly a one-hour drive from the skydiving resort.

KING: You're right, but…

QUEEN: It could be one of the European tourists who come to the skydiving resort.

KING: But she could have stayed to tell me her name.

QUEEN: Do you want to broadcast for any girl who helped you to come forward? But then anybody could come along and say it was she who saved you. Oh, here comes Rakim. Hello my son. Where have you been? Your father has been looking for you, and have you eaten.

RAKIM: I'm not hungry. I'm looking for Sandra and Joyce. They are no longer at the royal guesthouse. Papa, what have you done or said to them?

KING: I asked them to go and I gave them money and tickets, so I thought they might have left by now, but I'm confused because someone saved me while I was falling from the sky one hour ago and the airport is totally on the other side of the city.

RAKIM: Yes, it was Sandra who saved you, I imagine. I must look for her. She has saved me in the same fashion before, and please, both of you, say nothing about her ability to anybody. Now, I must go look for her, and thank you Papa for driving out the love of my life.

[Before his father can speak, Rakim is already gone.]

KING: But he can't marry her. Tradition doesn't allow him to marry a foreigner as his first wife.

QUEEN: What tradition? If it was the other girl who saved you, you would marry her.

KING: Yes, but as a second wife because this is allowed in the tradition. A king or prince can marry a foreigner as his second wife.

QUEEN: You're the king, so you can change the tradition or rewrite the constitution.

KING: But why should I rewrite the constitution?

QUEEN: For the love of your son and for the young woman who saved the life of the king.

KING: But he can marry an indigenous as his first wife and marry her later as second wife.

QUEEN: Maybe he doesn't want another wife, just this girl Sandra.

KING: But tradition…

QUEEN: It's a stupid and old tradition.

KING: Look woman, don't insult the constitution of the land.

QUEEN: Think of your son's happiness and your life being saved. What are theses things compared to your old ways?

[The Queen goes inside and the King is left alone. He does some deep thinking and decides to change or add to the constitution. He calls the chief adviser and the lawmakers and asks them to add to the constitution that anyone who saves the king's life, be he or she an indigenous person or not, will be treated as royalty. The constitution is amended with this phrase, and Rakim can now marry Sandra without marrying a second wife.]

KING: Guard, help Prince Rakim look for his guest, and call the airport to check if these women have left the country.

[The queen takes some of the palace guard and hurries to the area where the king always does his sky diving. She goes to the highest hotel and asks the front desk clerk to give her the names of

every guest that checked into the hotel in the last 6 hours. The waiter tells her that during the last 6 hours just two men and two women checked in. The queen asks for the room number of the two girls. The queen immediately goes up to their room and knocks on the door. They open the door and immediately the palace guard introduces the queen of the land, the queen asks the palace guard to stay outside while she speaks with the girls.]

QUEEN: Hello.

SANDRA: I'm Sandra and she's Joyce.

JOYCE: Why can't you people just leave us alone, or does the law or tradition not permit us to stay in this country today at all? Look, we still have visas to stay for one month, and right now we would like to contact our nearest consulate.

QUEEN [*laughing*]: No need for that.

SANDRA: Why not?

JOYCE: Look, we've got a right to let our people know what treatment we're facing here.

QUEEN: Both the king and I are very sorry for everything that has happened. It is just an…

JOYCE: Okay, just leave us alone.

QUEEN: I'll leave you alone if I can, but Rakim and the king want you to come back.

SANDRA: After all the King said and after Rakim himself did not even care to come to our defence?

QUEEN: Rakim did not come because he got into an argument with the king about you and out of confusion and frustration he ran out of the palace.

SANDRA: I hope nothing has happened to him.

JOYCE: And where is he now?

QUEEN: He is running all over the place looking for you two. Please come back. Don't leave. My son really loves you.

JOYCE: But his father said Rakim, by tradition or law, must not associate himself with someone like us.

QUEEN: The king has changed that phrase in our tradition. It's an old tradition, and now the king and I want Sandra to be Rakim's wife.

SANDRA: But…

JOYCE: Yes, but the king called us names.

QUEEN: On behalf of the king, I say we are both sorry for any insults. Please, come with me. Don't make Rakim do something stupid, as I can see he loves you dearly Sandra and I think you love him too.

JOYCE: Well…

QUEEN: Please. [*The Queen now holds Sandra and Joyce both by the hand.*] Please come back with me. Don't make Rakim do…

SANDRA: Okay, I'll come for Rakim's sake.

JOYCE: Yes, just for Rakim's sake, but you are such a nice queen.

QUEEN: I'm happy you two are coming back home to Rakim.

[They go back to the royal palace and the queen plans to give the king and Rakim a surprise, so she asks Sandra and Joyce to hide inside. When the king comes back, he is very angry with his guards and promises to sack the airport staff for not knowing if the girls have left or not. He is shouting at his guards when Rakim comes back into the palace in accompanied by his own guards and his cousin, Prince Jokin. Rakim starts crying in front of his parents. His mother goes to him, holds him by the shoulder, and his father shouts at him to stop crying and to behave like a true successor to the throne. As the next king, his father tells him, he must not cry about a woman in public.]

KING: Look Rakim, stop this crying now.

QUEEN: Let him cry. He is in love.

KING: But tradition says the prince doesn't cry in

public because it's assumed he gets everything he needs.

QUEEN: You and your tradition. Look tradition would have made us let our child lose the love of his life.

JOKIN: Would have? I've got Masters degree in English, and I know when you use "would have" that all is not lost.

[From behind the curtain where the Queen asked Sandra and Joyce to hide, they have heard the entire discussion. Joyce whispers to Sandra that this other guy who just spoke is very intelligent, and he said he has got a Masters degree in English. And, she says, he is cute as well.]

SANDRA: Joyce, don't tell me you are already crazy for him.

JOYCE: You've got the prince, so I think I should have his friend.

SANDRA: How do you know he is his friend?

JOYCE: Look how he stands close to Rakim and the queen, and there is obviously a difference between him and the guards. And he is wearing royal dress.

SANDRA: This may be the traditional clothing here and he may be married anyway.

JOYCE: I'll wait until the show is over so that I can hear about him some more.

[Rakim is no longer weeping.]

RAKIM: Papa, it's your fault they left.

KING: Yes, but my queen needs to explain her "would have."

QUEEN: Maybe they are at the sky diving resort area. Did anyone check there?

GUARDS: No.

KING: I'll deal with all of you for your incompetence. You should know to check there without been told.

QUEEN: What do they do now?

KING: Now you can take the helicopter to the sky diving resort and check every hotel there for the girls.

RAKIM: Wait guards. I'll come along.

KING: No, you wait here.

QUEEN: Let him go, but let me give him something that will bring him luck first.

KING: You with your lucky leaf again, but I hope it works this time.

QUEEN: It has worked already. I gave it to him when he went to Europe and now he has found himself a wife.

RAKIM: Mother, please be quick. There is no time to waste.

KING: Please hurry up before they leave.

QUEEN: Okay, here is my luck.

[The Queen opens the curtain, and Sandra and Joyce come out, both gorgeously dressed in royal outfits. Rakim runs quickly to Sandra and they embrace each other and kiss for a long moment. Jokin says hi Joyce, and finally Rakim and Sandra let loose of each other.]

RAKIM: Sandra, meet my cousin Jokin. Jokin, this is Sandra and Joyce.

JOKIN: Pleased to meet you two.

JOYCE: You are very intelligent to figure out what "would have" meant in the Queen's speech.

JOKIN: Oh, you heard it all?

RAKIM: Come all, let me introduce you to my parents officially.

KING: No need for official introductions. She is accepted as part of us. Let the palace workers prepare the palace for a big celebration.

RAKIM: Wait Papa. I want to introduce to you to the woman I want to marry.

KING: Em…em…

QUEEN: What is this em… em for?

KING: Em is for engaged, and please get married with all my blessing.

[Rakim embraces his father and mother, and

the whole palace is soon filled with fanfare and celebration

The wedding is planned and Sandra invites her people from Europe. After the marriage Joyce goes back to Europe and is always in contact with Jokin, who later comes to Europe to see Joyce. They are together much now, and one day Jokin asks Joyce if she would marry him. Joyce says yes. In no time they get married and Joyce goes back with Jokin to the Far East.

www.ingramcontent.com/pod-product-compliance
Ingram Content Group UK Ltd.
Pitfield, Milton Keynes, MK11 3LW, UK
UKHW040015200726
13854UKWH00001B/221

9 781553 952008